THE WAR ON AI

DEEPFAKES AND

DISINFORMATION

Artificial Intelligence Solutions to Combat Deepfake Disinformation

ENZO MILANO

The War on AI Deepfakes and Disinformation

Artificial Intelligence Solutions to Combat Deepfake Disinformation

ENZO MILANO

Table of Contents

Introduction

Deepfakes are a form of disinformation that utilizes artificial intelligence (AI) to create manipulated media, such as images, videos, or audio, that appear to be real but have actually been fabricated or altered. This technology has the potential to be particularly convincing and damaging, as it can create fake content that is nearly indistinguishable from real content.

Deepfakes have already been used in various ways, including in the context of elections and political discourse. For example, during the 2020 US presidential election, a deepfake video was created that showed presidential candidate Joe Biden appearing to say something that he had never actually said. The video was shared on social media and quickly went viral, leading to concerns about the potential impact on the election.

Similarly, deepfakes have been used to spread misinformation and propaganda in other contexts. For example, during the COVID-19 pandemic, a deepfake video was created that appeared to show a government official discussing a conspiracy theory about the origins of the virus. The video was widely shared and believed to be real, despite being completely fabricated.

The use of deepfakes in disinformation campaigns poses a significant threat to individual and societal resilience. By creating fake content that is nearly indistinguishable from real content, deepfakes have the potential to erode trust in institutions, media, and even our own senses. This can lead to confusion, mistrust, and polarization, which can have serious consequences for democracy and the rule of law.

To mitigate the risks associated with deepfakes, it is essential to develop strategies for detecting and debunking fake content. This may involve investing in AI-powered tools that can identify deepfakes, as well as promoting media literacy and critical thinking skills among the general public. Additionally, social media platforms and other online intermediaries must take responsibility for preventing the spread of deepfakes on their platforms, and governments must consider regulations and laws to prohibit the use of deepfakes in disinformation campaigns.

Deepfake technology, which enables the creation of synthetically altered footage, has become a growing concern due to its potential to spread disinformation and harm individuals. The technology allows for the digitally modification of a person's face or body to appear as someone or something else, creating increasingly lifelike videos. This has raised fears about the potential for foreign and domestic disinformation, as well as the exploitation of individuals through AI-enabled pornography sites (Jankowicz et al., 2021).

The use of deepfake technology has already been observed in various instances, including political disinformation and harassment. For example, during the 2020 US presidential election, a deepfake video was created that appeared to show presidential candidate Joe Biden saying something that he had never actually said (Merriam-Webster, undated-a). The video was shared on social media and quickly went viral, leading to concerns about the potential impact on the election.

Moreover, deepfake technology has also been used to create AI-enabled pornography sites, which have targeted women and other marginalized groups (Jankowicz et al., 2021). These sites use deepfake technology to create synthetic videos that appear to show individuals engaging in sexual acts, often without their consent. This has raised serious concerns about privacy, consent, and the exploitation of individuals through technology.

To address these concerns, it is essential to develop strategies for detecting and mitigating the impact of deepfake technology. This may involve investing in AI-powered tools that can identify deepfakes, as well as promoting media literacy and critical thinking skills among the general public. Additionally, social media platforms and other online intermediaries must take responsibility for preventing the spread of deepfakes on their platforms, and governments must consider regulations and laws to prohibit the use of deepfakes in disinformation campaigns.

The threat posed by deepfake technology highlights the need for a comprehensive approach to addressing disinformation and promoting media literacy in the digital age. By staying ahead of the curve in terms of technology and critical thinking skills, we can better protect ourselves and our societies from the harmful effects of disinformation.

The threat posed by deepfakes highlights the need for a comprehensive approach to addressing disinformation and promoting media literacy in the digital age. By staying ahead of the curve in terms of technology and critical thinking skills, we can better protect ourselves and our societies from the harmful effects of disinformation.

In other ways, however, the potential for havoc is yet to be realized. For example, some commentators expressed confidence that the 2020 election would be targeted and potentially upended by a deepfake video. Although the deepfakes did not come, that does not eliminate the risk for future elections (Simonite, 2020)

Deepfake technology has the potential to cause significant harm in various ways, including the manipulation of visual media to spread misinformation and disrupt democratic processes. The 2020 US presidential election was a prime example of this, as there were concerns that deepfake videos could be used to manipulate public opinion and sway voters. Although no such deepfakes were detected during the election, the risk of their use in future elections remains a concern (Simonite, 2020).

The potential for deepfakes to disrupt democratic processes is not limited to elections. They can also be used to manipulate public opinion and sway policy decisions. For example, a deepfake video could be created to make it appear as though a political leader made a statement that they never actually made, potentially leading to a breakdown in international relations or a misguided policy decision.

Moreover, deepfakes can also be used to spread misinformation and propaganda. With the ability to create convincing videos that appear to show real events, deepfakes can be used to create fake news stories or propaganda campaigns that are designed to manipulate public opinion. This can have serious consequences, such as the spread of conspiracy theories and propaganda campaigns that can lead to social unrest and violence.

The potential for deepfakes to cause harm is not limited to the political sphere. They can also be used to manipulate individuals and communities, leading to personal and emotional harm. For example, deepfakes can be used to create revenge porn, where intimate images or videos of individuals are manipulated and shared without their consent. Similarly, deepfakes can be used to create fake videos that damage an individual's reputation or lead to harassment and bullying.

The potential for deepfakes to cause harm is vast and varied. From manipulating democratic processes to spreading misinformation and propaganda, to causing personal and emotional harm, the risks associated with deepfakes are significant. It is essential that we take steps to mitigate these risks and ensure that deepfakes are used responsibly and ethically. This may include developing regulations and laws to govern the use of deepfakes, investing in technology to detect and prevent their use, and educating the public about the potential dangers of deepfakes. By taking these steps, we can minimize the risks associated with deepfakes and ensure that they are used for positive and beneficial purposes.

The rise of deepfakes and other forms of AI-generated fake content arrives at a time when the importance of truth is already in decline in American society, according to a report by RAND colleagues Jennifer Kavanagh and Michael D. Rich. The report highlights four key trends that contribute to this decline:

1. Increasing disagreement over facts and analytical interpretations: There is a growing divide in how people evaluate facts and interpret data, leading to increased disagreement and mistrust.

2. Blurring the line between opinion and fact: The distinction between opinion and fact is becoming increasingly blurred, with opinion often being presented as fact and vice versa.

3. Increase in the relative volume and influence of opinion over fact: The volume and influence of opinion are increasing, while the importance of factual information is declining.

4. Declining trust in respected sources of factual information: Trust in sources of factual information, such as the media and academic institutions, is decreasing.

These trends suggest that deepfakes and other forms of AI-generated fake content will find a highly susceptible audience, as people are increasingly open to information that confirms their pre-existing beliefs and biases. This creates a fertile ground for the spread of misinformation and disinformation, which can have serious consequences for society.

The purpose of this book is to provide an overview of the deepfake threat. The Perspective first presents a review of the technology undergirding deepfakes and associated AI-driven technologies that provide the foundation for deepfake videos, voice cloning, deepfake images, and generative text. It highlights the threats that deepfakes pose, as well as factors that could mitigate such threats. The paper then provides a review of the ongoing efforts to detect and counter deepfakes and concludes with an overview of recommendations for policymakers. This Perspective is based on a review of published literature on deepfake- and AI-disinformation technologies. Moreover, over the course of writing this Perspective, I consulted 12 leading experts in the disinformation field.

Artificial Intelligence Systems

Deepfake technology, which enables the creation of manipulated videos, audio, and images that appear authentic, has gained significant attention in recent years due to its potential use in disinformation campaigns. However, other AI technologies, such as voice cloning, deepfake images, and generative text, also pose a significant threat to the spread of misinformation. In this section, we will review the technologies and capabilities undergirding these AI-based disinformation tools.

1. Deepfake Videos: Deepfake videos use machine learning algorithms to manipulate existing videos by superimposing new content, such as a different face or voice, onto the original footage. This creates a convincing illusion that the manipulated video is authentic. Deepfake videos have already been used in various applications, including entertainment, advertising, and politics. However, their potential use in disinformation campaigns has raised concerns about their impact on society.

2. Voice Cloning: Voice cloning technology uses machine learning algorithms to mimic the voice of a person, creating a virtual voice that sounds like the original voice. This technology has various applications, such as voice acting, voiceovers, and language learning. However, it can also be used to create fake audio recordings that appear authentic, potentially leading to misinformation.

3. Deepfake Images: Deepfake images use machine learning algorithms to manipulate existing images by superimposing new content onto the original image. This can create convincing fake images that are difficult to distinguish from authentic images. Deepfake images can be used in various ways, such as creating fake news articles, propaganda, or doctored photographs.

4. Generative Text: Generative text technology uses machine learning algorithms to generate text that appears to be written by a human. This technology has various applications, such as content generation, chatbots,

and language translation. However, it can also be used to create fake news articles, propaganda, or other forms of misinformation.

The capabilities undergirding these AI-based disinformation tools are rapidly advancing, making it increasingly difficult to distinguish between authentic and manipulated content. For instance, deepfake technology has improved significantly in recent years, with some deepfake videos becoming almost indistinguishable from authentic videos. Similarly, voice cloning technology has become increasingly sophisticated, with some voice clones sounding almost identical to the original voice.

The use of these AI technologies in disinformation campaigns poses a significant threat to society. For example, deepfake videos can be used to create fake news videos that spread misinformation, or to create propaganda videos that manipulate public opinion. Voice cloning technology can be used to create fake audio recordings that spread false information or propaganda. Deepfake images can be used to create fake news articles or propaganda posters that are convincing and difficult to distinguish from authentic content. Generative text technology can be used to create fake news articles or propaganda texts that are convincing and coherent.

The use of AI technologies in disinformation campaigns represents a significant threat to society. The capabilities undergirding these technologies are rapidly advancing, making it increasingly difficult to distinguish between authentic and manipulated content. It is essential for individuals, organizations, and governments to be aware of these technologies and their potential use in disinformation campaigns, and to take steps to mitigate their impact. This includes developing tools and techniques to detect and identify manipulated content, as well as educating the public about the potential dangers of AI-based disinformation.

Deepfake Videos

Generative Adversarial Networks (GANs) are a type of deep learning algorithm used to generate synthetic data, such as images or videos, that are nearly indistinguishable from real data. The key to GANs is the use of two neural networks: a generator and a discriminator.

The generator is a neural network that takes a random noise input and generates a synthetic image or video output. The goal of the generator is to produce images or videos that are indistinguishable from real data.

The discriminator is also a neural network that takes an image or video input and outputs a probability that the input is real or fake. The goal of the discriminator is to correctly identify real and fake images or videos.

During training, the generator and discriminator are trained simultaneously. The generator tries to produce images or videos that can fool the discriminator into thinking they are real, while the discriminator tries to correctly identify real and fake images or videos. This adversarial process leads to the generator producing higher and higher quality synthetic data, as it tries to outsmart the discriminator.

Once the GAN is trained, the generator can be used to produce synthetic data that is nearly indistinguishable from real data. This data can be used for a variety of purposes, such as in deepfake videos, where the faces or bodies of individuals in a video are altered to create a synthetic video that appears real.

The use of GANs in deepfake videos has led to a significant increase in the quality of the synthetic data produced. The videos created using GANs are highly realistic and can be used to create fake news, propaganda, or other forms of disinformation.

However, it's important to note that GANs can also be used for positive purposes, such as in entertainment, advertising, and education. The technology itself is neutral, and its use depends on the intentions of those who employ it.

GANs are a powerful tool for generating synthetic data, including deepfake videos. The adversarial process between the generator and discriminator leads to high-quality synthetic data that can be used for various purposes. While the technology has the potential to be misused, it also has many positive applications that can benefit society.

The advent of Deepfake technology has spawned a new era of video manipulation, enabling the creation of increasingly convincing fake videos. In 2014, Ian Goodfellow and his colleagues introduced the Generative Adversarial Networks (GANs) system, which has since revolutionized the field of video manipulation.

One notable example of the alarming progression of deepfake technology is the TikTok account of a user named Tom (@deeptomcruise), who posted a series of deepfake videos in spring 2021. These videos appeared to feature Tom Cruise speaking, and they quickly amassed over 15.9 million views. The videos were so realistic that they sparked widespread concern about the potential for deepfake disinformation.

The Tom Cruise deepfake videos were created using advanced GANs, which enabled the manipulation of the video's visual and audio elements. The AI-powered algorithm used in the creation of these videos has the ability to learn from the input data and generate new, synthetic data that appears authentic. In this case, the algorithm was trained on a large dataset of Tom Cruise's interviews and speeches, allowing it to generate a convincing imitation of the actor's voice and mannerisms.

The release of these deepfake videos has raised alarm bells among experts and the general public, as they demonstrate the ease with which AI technology can be used to manipulate and deceive. The potential for such technology to be used in disinformation campaigns or political propaganda is a cause for concern, as it could lead to a loss of trust in video evidence and further erode the already fragile state of truth in the digital age.

In response to the growing threat of deepfake technology, researchers and experts are working to develop tools and techniques to detect and mitigate the effects of deepfakes. This includes the development of AI-powered algorithms that can identify manipulated videos and audio, as well as the creation of digital watermarks that can be used to verify the authenticity of digital media. Additionally, there is a growing focus on educating the public about the dangers of deepfakes and the importance of media literacy in the digital age.

The advent of deepfake technology has ushered in a new era of video manipulation, with the potential to revolutionize the way we consume and interact with digital media. However, it also poses significant risks, particularly in the realm of disinformation and manipulation. As such, it is crucial that we remain vigilant and proactive in our efforts to combat the negative effects of deepfakes and ensure that truth and authenticity remain a cornerstone of our digital landscape.

The creation of sophisticated deepfakes requires significant resources, including high-end computing equipment, a substantial amount of time, and a significant investment of money. The process also necessitates a skilled actor who can accurately mimic the movements and mannerisms of the person being depicted.

To create realistic deepfakes, a large amount of authentic footage must be inputted into AI models to train them. This process can be time-consuming, requiring weeks or even months to complete. The training process itself can also be computationally intensive, requiring powerful graphics processing units (GPUs) to handle the complex algorithms involved.

For example, the deepfakes created by @deeptomcruise required the use of two NVIDIA RTX 8000 GPUs, which cost upward of $5,795 each. The developers also had to carefully review the final footage frame by frame to identify and correct any noticeable tells, such as awkward or non-lifelike eye movements.

In addition to the technical aspects of creating deepfakes, the process also requires a talented actor who can successfully mimic the movements and mannerisms of the person being depicted. This requires a deep understanding of the person's behavior, mannerisms, and speech patterns, as well as the ability to accurately replicate them.

The creation of sophisticated deepfakes is a complex and resource-intensive process that requires significant investments of time, money, and skill.

The advent of deepfake technology has led to a significant improvement in the quality of synthetic videos over time. The early deepfakes, such as the 2018 deepfake of Barack Obama using profanity (Vincent, 2018) and the 2020 deepfake of a Richard Nixon speech that Nixon never gave (MIT Open Learning, 2020), were not as sophisticated as the Tom Cruise deepfakes. However, with each passing iteration, the quality of the videos has become increasingly lifelike, making it more challenging to detect the synthetic components with the naked eye.

The improvement in quality is attributed to advancements in machine learning algorithms, particularly generative adversarial networks (GANs), which are used to create deepfakes. GANs consist of two neural networks: a generator and a discriminator. The generator creates synthetic data, while the discriminator evaluates the generated data and provides feedback to the generator. This feedback loop enables the generator to improve over time, resulting in more realistic synthetic data.

Furthermore, the development of deepfake technology has led to a decrease in the cost of creating such videos. As the technology becomes more widely available, the cost of producing high-quality deepfakes is likely to decrease, making it more accessible to a broader range of individuals and organizations.

In addition, the availability of large datasets and advancements in computer vision have made it possible to create deepfakes with less training footage. This has opened up new possibilities for creating deepfakes of individuals who may not have a large amount of publicly available footage, such as historical figures or private individuals.

The advancements in deepfake technology have led to a significant improvement in the quality of synthetic videos, making them increasingly lifelike and difficult to detect with the naked eye. As the technology continues to evolve, it is likely that deepfakes will become even more sophisticated and convincing, with potential applications in various fields, such as entertainment, education, and marketing.

The rise of deepfake technology has led to a proliferation of webpages offering deepfake services, allowing users to create convincing and often disturbing manipulations of reality. One such service is Reface, which allows users to swap faces with faces in existing videos and GIFs, creating the illusion that the user is in the video themselves. Another popular service is MyHeritage, which animates photos of deceased relatives, creating a digital representation of the deceased that can be interacted with.

However, not all deepfake services are benign. The Chinese app Zao, created by Changsha Shenduronghe Network Technology, allows users to impose their own face over one from a selection of movie characters, raising concerns about the potential for misuse. For example, users could create deepfakes of themselves in compromising or illegal situations, or use the technology to impersonate others for malicious purposes.

Perhaps the most notorious example of a deepfake service is DeepNude, which allows users to upload photos, primarily of women, and delivers an output in which the photo subject appears to be nude. This service has sparked outrage and concern about the potential for exploitation and harassment. Other webpages offer similar services, further highlighting the need for greater regulation and oversight of deepfake technology.

While deepfake technology has the potential to revolutionize industries such as entertainment and advertising, it also poses significant risks and challenges. As the use of deepfakes becomes more widespread, it is essential that we address these concerns and develop appropriate regulations and safeguards to prevent the misuse of this technology.

Voice Cloning

Voice cloning, a technology that allows for the creation of a synthetic voice that mimics a real person's voice, is another way in which deepfakes are used. This technology has been used in various online and phone apps, such as Celebrity Voice Cloning (Hobantay Inc., undated) and Voicer Famous AI Voice Changer (Voloshchuk, undated), which allow users to mimic the voices of popular celebrities.

However, the use of voice cloning technology has also raised concerns about its potential for misuse. For example, in one instance, the CEO of a UK-based energy firm reported receiving a phone call from a person claiming to be the CEO of a large technology company, who requested a meeting to discuss a potential business partnership. The call was later discovered to be a deepfake, created using voice cloning technology, and the intended target was likely the CEO's personal information or company data.

This incident highlights the potential risks associated with voice cloning technology, particularly in the context of social engineering attacks. Deepfakes can be used to create convincing phone calls, emails, or messages that appear to come from a trusted source, but are actually malicious attempts to gather sensitive information or manipulate individuals.

Moreover, voice cloning technology can also be used to spread misinformation or propaganda. For example, a deepfake audio or video recording of a political leader or public figure can be created to make it seem like they are saying something they never actually said, or to manipulate their words to fit a certain agenda. This can have serious consequences, such as fueling conspiracy theories, sowing confusion or mistrust, or even inciting violence.

To mitigate these risks, it is essential to develop robust methods for detecting and mitigating deepfakes, as well as to raise public awareness about the potential dangers of this technology. Additionally, policymakers and regulators must consider the ethical implications of voice cloning technology and work to establish guidelines and regulations that prevent its misuse.

Voice cloning technology has been used in various scams and fraudulent activities, including the two examples you've mentioned. In the first case, the CEO of a UK-based energy firm was tricked into executing a wire transfer of €220,000 to a Hungarian supplier's bank account, allegedly after receiving a phone call from a voice that was cloned to sound like the CEO of a large technology company. The caller claimed to be the CEO of the technology company and requested a meeting to discuss a potential business partnership. The CEO, believing the call to be legitimate, transferred the money as requested.

In the second case, a man in Philadelphia alleged that he was the victim of a voice-cloning attack. He reportedly received a phone call from a voice that sounded like his son, claiming that he was in jail and needed money for a lawyer. The man, believing the voice to be his son, wired US$9,000 to a stranger's bank account.

These incidents highlight the potential risks associated with voice cloning technology. By creating a synthetic voice that mimics a real person's voice, scammers and fraudsters can trick individuals into divulging sensitive information or transferring large sums of money. The technology can be used to create convincing phone calls, emails, or messages that appear to come from a trusted source, but are actually malicious attempts to manipulate individuals.

The use of voice cloning technology in these scams and fraudulent activities has serious implications for individuals and organizations. It is essential to be aware of the potential risks associated with this technology and to take steps to protect yourself from being targeted. This includes being cautious when receiving unsolicited phone calls or messages, particularly those that request personal information or money transfers.

It is also important to use robust security measures, such as two-factor authentication, to verify the identity of the person or organization on the other end of the communication.

Voice cloning technology has the potential to be used in various malicious ways, including scams and fraudulent activities. It is important to be aware of the risks associated with this technology and to take steps to protect yourself from being targeted. By staying vigilant and using robust security measures, individuals and organizations can minimize the risk of falling victim to these types of attacks.

Deepfake Images

Deepfake images, specifically those in the form of headshot photos, have become a cause for concern due to their ability to appear remarkably human and lifelike. These images are readily accessible through certain websites, such as Generated Photos (undated), which allow users to quickly and easily construct fake headshots.

The ease of accessibility and creation of deepfake images has raised alarm bells in various industries, including law enforcement, journalism, and entertainment. The potential for these images to be used in fraudulent activities, such as identity theft or propaganda campaigns, is a significant concern.

For instance, deepfake images could be used to create fake profiles on social media or dating websites, leading to identity theft or other forms of deception. They could also be used to create fake news articles or propaganda campaigns, further contributing to the spread of misinformation.

Moreover, the use of deepfake images in the entertainment industry has also raised ethical concerns. For example, the use of deepfake technology to create fake movie or TV scenes could lead to the manipulation of audience emotions, blurring the lines between reality and fiction.

To mitigate these concerns, it is crucial to develop robust methods for detecting and mitigating deepfake images. This includes the development of advanced algorithms that can identify and flag fake images, as well as increased public awareness and education about the dangers of deepfakes.

Additionally, policymakers and regulators must consider the ethical implications of deepfake technology and work to establish guidelines and regulations that prevent its misuse. This includes ensuring that deepfake technology is not used to manipulate public opinion or propagate misinformation.

The responsible use of deepfake technology requires a multifaceted approach that balances its potential benefits with the need to protect society from its potential risks. By staying vigilant and taking proactive measures, we can ensure that deepfake technology is used for the betterment of society, rather than to its detriment.

The use of deepfake technology is concerning because it suggests that state-run espionage operations are utilizing advanced technology to create fake online identities and gather information. The fact that the profile was connected to a small but influential network of accounts, including a government official, highlights the potential for deepfakes to be used in targeted attacks against individuals or organizations.

The discovery of this deepfake profile also underscores the need for increased vigilance in the digital age. As technology continues to advance, it is becoming increasingly easier for individuals and organizations to create convincing fake identities and content. It is essential that we remain aware of these developments and take steps to protect ourselves and our organizations from the potential threats posed by deepfakes.

One way to mitigate the risks associated with deepfakes is to implement robust security measures, such as two-factor authentication and regular password changes. Additionally, it is important to be cautious when interacting with unfamiliar profiles or accounts, particularly those that request personal information or access.

Another key aspect of protecting ourselves from deepfakes is to cultivate a healthy dose of skepticism when consuming online content. We should be wary of information that seems too good (or bad) to be true and be willing to fact-check and verify the authenticity of content before sharing it with others.

Finally, it is essential to stay informed about the latest advancements in deepfake technology and their potential applications. By remaining aware of the risks and challenges associated with deepfakes, we can take proactive steps to protect ourselves and our organizations from their potential threats.

Deepfake images have also increasingly been used as part of fake social media accounts. In one of the first large-scale discoveries of this phenomenon, Facebook found dozens of state-sponsored accounts that used such fake images as profile photos (Nimmo et al., 2019).2 One might suspect that the use of deepfake images in fake social media accounts is a new tactic employed by state actors to spread disinformation and propaganda.

The use of deepfake images in fake social media accounts poses a significant threat to individuals' privacy and security. These fake accounts can be used to gather personal information, spread malware, or steal sensitive data. Additionally, deepfake images can be used to create fake profiles that are indistinguishable from real ones, making it challenging to identify and flag fake accounts.

The use of deepfake images in fake social media accounts also highlights the need for increased vigilance in the digital age. As technology continues to advance, it is becoming increasingly easier for individuals and organizations to create convincing fake identities and content. Therefore, it is essential to remain aware of these developments and take steps to protect ourselves and our organizations from the potential threats posed by deepfakes.

To mitigate the risks associated with deepfake images in fake social media accounts, it is crucial to be cautious when interacting with unfamiliar profiles or accounts. We should be wary of profiles that seem too good (or bad) to be true and be willing to fact-check and verify the authenticity of content before sharing it with others. Additionally, social media platforms must take responsibility for monitoring and flagging fake accounts, and governments must consider regulations to prevent the misuse of deepfake technology.

The use of deepfake images in fake social media accounts is a growing concern that requires immediate attention. We must remain vigilant and take proactive steps to protect ourselves and our organizations from the potential threats posed by deepfakes. By staying informed and taking the necessary precautions, we can prevent the misuse of deepfake technology and ensure our online safety and security.

The use of fake images in propaganda campaigns can be attributed to the desire to avoid detection and attribution. Propagandists aim to create a convincing narrative that is free from suspicion, and the use of stolen images can raise red flags and undermine the credibility of the message. By creating fake images, propagandists can circumvent the risk of being traced back to the source and maintain a level of anonymity.

Moreover, the use of fake images allows propagandists to manipulate public opinion without being held accountable. In the digital age, images have become an indispensable tool for shaping public opinion and influencing political discourse. Propagandists can exploit this by creating fake images that are designed to elicit emotions and sway public opinion in a particular direction. By doing so, they can create a false narrative that is difficult to challenge or refute.

Another reason why propagandists might prefer to use fake images is that they can be custom-made to suit a specific purpose. Unlike stolen images, which may not always align with the intended message, fake images can be tailored to fit the desired narrative. This allows propagandists to create a more cohesive and persuasive message, which can be particularly effective in influencing public opinion.

Furthermore, the use of fake images can also be seen as a way to evade the legal and ethical implications of using stolen images. Propagandists who use stolen images risk being exposed and held accountable for their actions, which can damage their reputation and undermine their credibility. In contrast, the use of fake images allows them to avoid these risks and maintain a level of plausible deniability.

The use of fake images in propaganda campaigns is a deliberate choice made by propagandists to avoid detection, attribution, and accountability. By creating fake images, propagandists can manipulate public opinion, evade legal and ethical implications, and maintain a level of anonymity. It is essential to be aware of these tactics and develop strategies to identify and expose propaganda campaigns that rely on fake images.

Generative Text

The use of natural language computer models to generate artificial yet lifelike text has been a topic of interest in recent years. In September 2020, the Guardian published an article titled "A Robot Wrote This Entire Article. Are You Scared Yet, Human?" which was generated using a language generator called Generative Pre-Trained Transformer-3 (GPT-3) developed by OpenAI. GPT-3 was trained on a large dataset that included information from various sources such as CommonCrawl, WebText, Wikipedia, and a corpus of books (Tom B. Brown et al., 2020).

The use of GPT-3 to generate the article sparked interest and discussion about the potential of AI to produce natural language text that is indistinguishable from human-written text. The article itself was written in a conversational style and addressed the topic of AI and its potential impact on human society. It also included quotes from experts in the field and even included a few jokes.

The ability of AI to generate natural language text has implications for various industries such as journalism, marketing, and customer service. However, it also raises questions about the role of human writers and the potential loss of jobs. Additionally, there are concerns about the ethical implications of using AI to generate fake news or propaganda.

The use of GPT-3 to generate the article in the Guardian highlights the rapid advancements being made in the field of natural language processing and the potential for AI to generate human-like text. It also underscores the need for ongoing discussions about the ethical and societal implications of such technologies.

The Guardian's experiment with GPT-3 highlights the impressive capabilities of language models in generating coherent and human-like text. By providing GPT-3 with a brief introductory paragraph and instructions to write a short op-ed, the editors at The Guardian were able to generate eight separate essays that were then combined to form a single article. The resulting text is remarkable in its clarity and coherence, and could easily be mistaken for a piece written by a human author.

The op-ed focuses on the theme of humans having nothing to fear from AI, a topic that has been the subject of much debate and discussion in recent years. GPT-3's essays argue that AI and humans can coexist peacefully, and that the fear of AI eradicating humanity is unfounded. The language used is simple and concise, making the arguments easy to follow and understand.

One of the key strengths of GPT-3's writing is its ability to maintain a consistent tone and style throughout the essays. The language is engaging and accessible, making it easy for readers to connect with the ideas being presented. Additionally, the essays demonstrate a clear understanding of the topic at hand, with GPT-3 providing logical and well-reasoned arguments to support its claims.

The fact that The Guardian's editors were able to cut and splice together eight separate essays to form a single article is a testament to the quality of GPT-3's writing. The text flows smoothly and naturally, with no indication that it was generated by a machine. This is a remarkable achievement, and one that highlights the rapidly advancing capabilities of language models like GPT-3.

The Guardian's experiment with GPT-3 demonstrates the exciting potential of language models to generate high-quality text that is indistinguishable from human-written content. As these models continue to evolve and improve, it will be fascinating to see how they are used to create new forms of writing and communication.

However, GPT-3 is not foolproof. A GPT-3–powered bot was let loose on a Reddit community,3 and it generated one post per minute for more than a week (Heaven, 2020). One post offered advice to formerly suicidal Reddit users, claiming that the poster was once suicidal but survived by relying on family and friends. Another user saw some of the posts and identified them as autogenerated (Heaven, 2020).

The fact that the GPT-3–powered bot was able to generate posts that were indistinguishable from those written by humans is a testament to the advanced capabilities of the language model. However, the fact that the bot was able to generate posts that were not accurate or truthful raises concerns about the potential misuse of such technology.

The use of GPT-3 to generate fake posts on Reddit highlights the need for vigilance in monitoring and regulating the use of AI language models. While these models can be incredibly useful for generating useful and informative content, they can also be used to spread misinformation and propaganda. It is important for social media platforms and other online communities to have measures in place to detect and prevent the use of AI-generated content that is harmful or deceptive.

Moreover, the incident also underscores the importance of transparency in the development and deployment of AI language models. It is crucial that the developers and users of these models are transparent about their capabilities and limitations, and that they take responsibility for ensuring that they are used ethically and responsibly.

While GPT-3 is an impressive language model that can generate human-like text, it is not foolproof and can be used to spread misinformation. It is important to be vigilant in monitoring and regulating the use of AI language models, and to ensure that they are used ethically and responsibly.

The concern about text-generation programs like GPT-3 being used by foreign adversaries to produce text-based propaganda at scale is a legitimate one. The use of such technology could potentially enable foreign actors to create large volumes of convincing and sophisticated propaganda content, without the need for human operators to draft it. This could be used to influence public opinion, sow discord, and undermine democratic institutions.

The use of GPT-2 software by FireEye researchers to replicate the kinds of divisive social media posts used by Russia's troll farm during the 2016 election is a prime example of this concern. The fact that a language model was able to generate content that was similar in style and tone to the propaganda produced by human operators is a testament to the advanced capabilities of these models.

The potential for AI-generated propaganda to be used in future elections and other democratic processes is a serious issue that needs to be addressed. It is important for governments, civil society organizations, and social media platforms to work together to detect and prevent the use of AI-generated propaganda, and to ensure that the public is aware of the potential risks and vulnerabilities associated with this technology.

Moreover, the development and deployment of AI-generated propaganda highlights the need for greater investment in media literacy education and critical thinking skills. It is essential that citizens are equipped with the skills and knowledge necessary to identify and debunk propaganda, regardless of whether it is generated by humans or AI.

The potential use of text-generation programs like GPT-3 for propaganda purposes is a significant concern that needs to be taken seriously. It is important for governments, civil society organizations, and social media platforms to work together to address this issue, and to ensure that the public is equipped with the skills and knowledge necessary to navigate the complex information landscape.

The use of barrage jamming tactics in information operations is a concern for democratic societies, as it can be used to overwhelm and manipulate public discourse. In the case of China's Xinjiang region, the Chinese government has been accused of using barrage jamming tactics to flood the online space with positive propaganda, in an attempt to drown out negative discussions about human rights abuses.

This tactic involves creating a large volume of content that is designed to dominate the online conversation and push negative stories down in search results. By creating a high volume of tweets, posts, and articles that are optimized for search engines, it becomes more difficult for people to find accurate and reliable information about the issue.

Barrage jamming can be particularly effective on social media platforms, where algorithms prioritize content that is popular and trending. By creating a large volume of content that is designed to go viral, it can be easy for propagandists to manipulate the online conversation and push their message to the top of the algorithmic feed.

The use of barrage jamming tactics is concerning because it can be used to manipulate public opinion and undermine democratic institutions. In the case of Xinjiang, the Chinese government's use of propaganda and disinformation has been criticized for its role in obscuring the reality of the situation and perpetuating human rights abuses.

To mitigate the risks associated with barrage jamming, it is important for social media platforms and other online communities to invest in moderation and fact-checking measures. This can include using artificial intelligence to identify and remove fake accounts and propaganda content, as well as partnering with independent fact-checking organizations to verify the accuracy of information. Additionally, it is important for individuals to remain vigilant and critical in their consumption of information, and to seek out multiple sources to verify the accuracy of what they are reading.

Barrage jamming is a concerning tactic that can be used to manipulate public discourse and undermine democratic institutions. It is important for social media platforms, fact-checking organizations, and individuals to work together to mitigate the risks associated with this tactic and ensure that accurate information is available to the public.

The use of text generators to create fake news articles or propaganda is a concerning trend that has the potential to spread misinformation and manipulate public opinion. The ability of these algorithms to generate high-quality, convincing content that mimics the style and tone of legitimate news sources poses a significant threat to the integrity of information online.

One of the main concerns with the use of text generators for propaganda is their ability to overwhelm genuine coverage of a particular story. By creating a large volume of fake news articles or social media posts that are optimized for search engines, it becomes increasingly difficult for people to find accurate and reliable information on a given topic. This can be particularly effective in situations where the fake news stories are designed to be sensational or inflammatory, as they may be more likely to capture people's attention and go viral.

Another concern is the potential for text generators to be used to spoof legitimate news sources, such as The New York Times. By creating fake articles that mimic the style and tone of real news articles, propagandists can create the illusion of legitimacy and credibility. This can be particularly effective in situations where the fake articles are designed to support a particular political or ideological agenda, as they may be more likely to be shared and believed by people who are already inclined to support that agenda.

Renée DiResta (2020) argues that the use of text generators for propaganda would help adversaries avoid the sloppy linguistic mistakes that human operators often make. This is a significant concern, as it means that the fake news stories generated by these algorithms may be more believable and difficult to detect than those created by human operators. This could make it more difficult for people to distinguish between real and fake news, and could further erode trust in the media and the information ecosystem as a whole.

To mitigate the risks associated with the use of text generators for propaganda, it is important for social media platforms, search engines, and other online communities to invest in moderation and fact-checking measures. This can include using artificial intelligence to identify and remove fake accounts and propaganda content, as well as partnering with independent fact-checking organizations to verify the accuracy of information. Additionally, it is important for individuals to remain vigilant and critical in their consumption of information, and to seek out multiple sources to verify the accuracy of what they are reading.

The use of text generators for propaganda is a concerning trend that has the potential to spread misinformation and manipulate public opinion. It is important for online communities and individuals to be aware of this trend and to take steps to mitigate its risks. By investing in moderation and fact-checking measures, and by remaining vigilant and critical in their consumption of information, we can work to ensure that accurate information is available to the public and that the integrity of the information ecosystem is maintained.

Risk and Implications

Risks

The risks associated with deepfakes and other forms of AI-generated content are numerous and varied, and can have significant impacts on both society and national security. Some potential risks include:

1. Misinformation and disinformation: Deepfakes can be used to create convincing but fake video footage that can be used to spread

misinformation or disinformation. This can be used to manipulate public opinion, sway political discourse, or even spread propaganda.

2. Identity theft: Deepfakes can be used to create fake videos that appear to be of a person, but are actually not. This can be used to impersonate individuals, commit fraud, or even blackmail people.

3. National security risks: Deepfakes can be used to create fake videos that appear to be of a political leader, military official, or other person of interest. This can be used to spread misinformation, sow discord, or even manipulate decision-making.

4. Erosion of trust: The proliferation of deepfakes can lead to a loss of trust in video footage, making it difficult to determine what is real and what is not. This can have serious consequences for society, as video footage is often used as evidence in legal proceedings, news reporting, and other important applications.

5. Unintended consequences: As deepfakes become more advanced, they can be used to create increasingly convincing but fake videos. This can lead to unintended consequences, such as the spread of false information, the manipulation of public opinion, or even violence.

6. Difficulty in detection: Deepfakes can be difficult to detect, making it challenging to determine whether a video is real or fake. This can lead to a situation where fake videos are accepted as real, with potentially serious consequences.

7. Malicious use: Deepfakes can be used maliciously, such as in the case of revenge porn, where fake videos are created to harm or embarrass someone.

8. Unregulated use: The use of deepfakes is largely unregulated, which means that there are few laws or guidelines governing their use. This can lead to a situation where deepfakes are used in ways that are harmful or unethical.

9. Ethical concerns: Deepfakes raise a number of ethical concerns, such as the potential for mass surveillance, the manipulation of public opinion, and the creation of fake news.

10. Unknown long-term effects: The long-term effects of deepfakes on society are not yet fully understood, and there is a need for further research to better understand their impacts.

The risks associated with deepfakes and other forms of AI-generated content are significant and far-reaching. It is important for society to be aware of these risks and to take steps to mitigate them, such as developing regulations and laws governing the use of deepfakes, investing in research to better understand their impacts, and educating the public about the potential dangers of deepfakes.

The article by Christoffer Waldemarsson (2020) highlights the potential risks associated with deepfakes, particularly in the context of elections. The author identifies four key ways in which deepfakes could be weaponized by adversaries or harmful actors:

1. Election manipulation: Deepfake content could be used to manipulate elections by creating fake videos that show a candidate engaging in nefarious or sexual acts or making controversial statements. The video could surface on the eve of a closely contested election, potentially swaying the outcome.

2. Propaganda: Deepfakes could be used to create propaganda videos that are designed to spread misinformation or fuel conspiracy theories. These videos could be used to manipulate public opinion, fuel political polarization, or even incite violence.

3. Fraud: Deepfakes could be used to commit fraud by creating fake videos that are used to defraud individuals or organizations. For example, a deepfake video could be used to impersonate a CEO or other high-level executive, convincing employees or investors to transfer large sums of money to fraudulent accounts.

4. Reputation destruction: Deepfakes could be used to destroy the reputation of individuals or organizations by creating fake videos that show them engaging in embarrassing or illegal activities. This could be used to discredit political opponents, silence activists, or ruin the reputation of businesses.

The article highlights the potential risks associated with deepfakes and the need for increased awareness and regulation to prevent their misuse. It emphasizes the importance of developing technologies and strategies to detect and mitigate deepfakes, as well as educating the public about their potential dangers.

The proliferation of deepfake content has the potential to significantly exacerbate social divisions in various ways. As mentioned, Russia has already utilized propaganda to exploit existing schisms within the U.S. public (Posard et al., 2020). Additionally, the increasing polarization of political discourse in the U.S. has resulted in individuals often employing propaganda-like tactics to discredit and attack those with opposing viewpoints.

The phenomenon of online echo chambers, where individuals primarily consume and share content that aligns with their existing beliefs, has been well-documented (Shin, 2020). The dissemination of partisan deepfakes and other AI-driven disinformation content can further reinforce these echo chambers, contributing to a more polarized and divided society.

The use of deepfakes in political discourse can have particularly detrimental effects. For instance, a deepfake video that appears to show a political candidate making an inflammatory statement or engaging in unethical behavior can quickly spread across social media, further entrenching existing biases and potentially swaying public opinion.

Moreover, the deployment of deepfakes in propaganda campaigns can be challenging to detect and mitigate, as they often exploit existing vulnerabilities in cognitive processing. Research has shown that individuals are more likely to accept and share information that aligns with their preexisting beliefs, making them more susceptible to manipulation by deepfakes and other forms of disinformation (Kull et al., 2018).

To address these concerns, it is crucial to develop and implement effective strategies for identifying and countering deepfakes. This includes investing in AI-powered detection tools, promoting media literacy programs, and fostering critical thinking skills among the public. Additionally, social media platforms and other online communities must take responsibility for monitoring and removing deepfake content from their platforms.

The combating of deepfakes and other forms of disinformation requires a multifaceted approach that involves government, civil society, and individual actors. By working together, we can reduce the negative impact of deepfakes on social divisions and promote a more informed and engaged citizenry.

The proliferation of deepfake content has the potential to significantly lower trust in institutions and authorities, as highlighted by Waldemarsson (2020). The manipulation of visual and audio content can be used to create fake videos, audio recordings, and images that appear to be real, but are actually fabricated. This can have devastating effects on trust in authorities, as well as on the reputation of individuals and organizations.

For instance, a deepfake video that appears to show a police officer acting violently could lead to widespread outrage and mistrust of law enforcement. Similarly, a fake video of a judge privately discussing ways to circumvent the judiciary system or border guards using racist language could further erode trust in the legal system and government institutions.

Such deepfakes can also undermine the credibility of real footage and evidence, making it more challenging for people to distinguish between fact and fiction. This can have serious consequences in various domains, such as journalism, law enforcement, and national security.

Moreover, the use of deepfakes can also perpetuate conspiracy theories and disinformation, further contributing to a breakdown of trust in institutions and authorities. As people become increasingly skeptical of the information they receive, they may turn to alternative sources that reinforce their existing beliefs, creating echo chambers that are resistant to fact-based information.

To mitigate the risks associated with deepfakes, it is essential to develop and implement effective strategies for detecting and mitigating disinformation. This includes investing in AI-powered detection tools, promoting media literacy programs, and fostering critical thinking skills among the public. Additionally, social media platforms and other online communities must take responsibility for monitoring and removing deepfake content from their platforms.

The combating of deepfakes and other forms of disinformation requires a multifaceted approach that involves government, civil society, and individual actors. By working together, we can reduce the negative impact of deepfakes on trust in institutions and authorities and promote a more informed and engaged citizenry.

The advent of deepfakes has the potential to significantly undermine journalism and trustworthy sources of information. With the ability to create highly believable fake videos, audio recordings, and images, even accurate content can be slandered as deepfakes by those who consider the content unfavorable. This phenomenon is referred to as the "liar's dividend" (Chesney and Citron, 2019).

The proliferation of deepfakes could lead to declining trust in prominent news institutions by sowing mistrust in even legitimate forms of news and information. As deepfakes become more sophisticated, it may become increasingly difficult for people to discern between real and fake content. This could lead to a situation where people become skeptical of all news and information, regardless of its accuracy.

Moreover, the use of deepfakes could also perpetuate conspiracy theories and disinformation. For example, a deepfake video could be created to make it appear as though a political leader made a statement that they never actually made. This could further contribute to the erosion of trust in institutions and the spread of misinformation.

The decline of trust in journalism and trustworthy sources of information could have serious consequences for society. It could lead to a loss of faith in the media, which is essential for holding those in power accountable and ensuring that the public is informed about important issues. It could also contribute to the spread of misinformation and the propagation of conspiracy theories, which could have serious consequences for public health, national security, and other areas of life.

To mitigate the risks associated with deepfakes, it is essential to develop and implement effective strategies for detecting and mitigating disinformation. This includes investing in AI-powered detection tools, promoting media literacy programs, and fostering critical thinking skills among the public. Additionally, social media platforms and other online communities must take responsibility for monitoring and removing deepfake content from their platforms.

The combating of deepfakes and other forms of disinformation requires a multifaceted approach that involves government, civil society, and individual actors. By working together, we can reduce the negative impact of deepfakes on trust in institutions and promote a more informed and engaged citizenry.

The consequences of deepfakes could be particularly severe in developing nations, where populations may have lower levels of education and literacy, live in more fragile democracies, and experience more interethnic strife. In these regions, various forms of disinformation and misinformation are already prevalent and have contributed to conflict and violence, such as the slaughter of Rohingya Muslims in Myanmar, violence against Muslims in India, and interethnic violence in Ethiopia. The use of deepfakes could exacerbate these negative consequences, further eroding trust in institutions and fueling hatred and violence.

In developing countries, the spread of deepfakes could be particularly dangerous due to the following factors:

1. Lower levels of education and literacy: In many developing countries, people may not have access to quality education, leaving them more susceptible to misinformation and disinformation. Deepfakes could further confuse people, making it difficult for them to distinguish between reality and fabricated content.

2. Fragile democracies: In some developing countries, democratic institutions are still in their infancy or are struggling to consolidate. The spread of deepfakes could weaken these institutions further, allowing authoritarian leaders to exploit the technology for their gain.

3. Interethnic strife: In many developing countries, tensions between different ethnic or religious groups are already high. Deepfakes could be used to stoke these tensions, creating an environment in which misinformation and disinformation can thrive.

4. Limited access to fact-checking resources: In some developing countries, people may not have access to fact-checking resources or independent media outlets that can help them verify information. This lack of access could make it difficult for people to distinguish between fact and fiction.

5. Limited technology literacy: In some developing countries, people may not be familiar with the latest technology, making it difficult for them to recognize deepfakes. This lack of familiarity could make it easier for people to be deceived by deepfakes.

To mitigate the risks associated with deepfakes in developing countries, it is essential to invest in media literacy programs, fact-checking initiatives, and technology education. Governments, civil society organizations, and technology companies must work together to ensure that people have the skills and resources they need to identify and combat disinformation.

Additionally, technology companies must take responsibility for monitoring and removing deepfake content from their platforms, and governments must create regulations that prevent the misuse of deepfakes.

The consequences of deepfakes could be devastating in developing countries, where vulnerable populations may be more susceptible to misinformation and disinformation. It is essential that we take proactive steps to address these risks and ensure that people have the tools they need to navigate the digital landscape safely.

The lack of resources and investment in content moderation and fact-checking efforts by social media companies, particularly in regions outside of the United States, is a significant concern. Facebook, for example, reportedly dedicates only 13% of its content moderation budget to consumers outside of the US (Frenkel and Davey, 2021). This lack of investment in regions with limited access to fact-checking resources and technology literacy could make it easier for deepfakes to spread misinformation and propaganda.

Moreover, other popular platforms in these regions, such as WhatsApp, have also been plagued with misinformation (Gursky, Riedl, and Woolley, 2021). The encrypted nature of WhatsApp makes it particularly challenging to monitor and remove misinformation, which could increase the likelihood that deepfakes go undetected in these regions.

The potential for deepfakes to spread misinformation and propaganda is particularly concerning in regions with limited access to fact-checking resources and technology literacy. In these regions, people may be more susceptible to believing false information and may have limited access to independent media outlets or fact-checking organizations that can verify the accuracy of information.

To address these concerns, social media companies must invest more resources in content moderation and fact-checking efforts in regions outside of the US. Additionally, governments and civil society organizations must work together to promote media literacy and critical thinking skills, particularly in regions with limited access to fact-checking resources and technology literacy.

Moreover, technology companies must also take responsibility for monitoring and removing misinformation from their platforms. This includes investing in AI-powered detection tools and partnering with independent fact-checking organizations to verify the accuracy of information.

A multifaceted approach that involves government, civil society, technology companies, and media literacy programs is necessary to address the challenges posed by deepfakes and ensure that people have access to accurate information. This will help to promote a more informed and engaged citizenry, which is essential for maintaining a healthy democracy.

The use of deepfakes and AI-generated media to manipulate and exploit women is a pressing concern, as it has the potential to exacerbate existing gender disparities in the realm of pornography. The production and dissemination of deepfake pornography, which often involves overlaying a selected face onto a pornography actor's body, can perpetuate the objectification and exploitation of women. This technology can be used to create convincing and damaging videos that are often created without the subject's consent, and can be used to abuse and exploit women in various ways.

Moreover, the use of deepfakes and AI-generated media can also pose broader national security threats. For instance, they could be used to embarrass, undermine, or exploit intelligence operatives, political candidates, journalists, or U.S. and allied leaders. The use of deepfakes in disinformation campaigns has already been observed, as in the case of a Russian-backed disinformation campaign that superimposed the face of a young Ukrainian parliamentarian, Svitlana Zalishchuk, onto pornographic images.

The proliferation of deepfake technology has the potential to amplify the harmful effects of pornography on women, particularly in the context of revenge porn, where intimate images or videos are shared without the subject's consent. The use of deepfakes to create fake pornographic content can make it more difficult to distinguish between real and fake content, which can further perpetuate the harm caused by revenge porn.

To address these concerns, it is essential to develop and implement policies that regulate the use of deepfakes and AI-generated media, particularly in the context of pornography and revenge porn. Additionally, educating the public about the dangers of deepfakes and the importance of media literacy can help mitigate the harm caused by these technologies. Furthermore, providing support and resources to victims of revenge porn and deepfake pornography is crucial in addressing the harm caused by these forms of exploitation.

The research community is still in the early stages of investigating the potential consequences of deepfakes. A systematic review of the scientific literature assessing the societal implications of deepfakes identified only 21 studies that used active experiments to understand the true impact of deepfakes on real users (Gamage, Chen, and Sasahara, 2021). The findings of these studies provide conflicting results regarding the ability of users to accurately detect deepfake videos and the degree to which such videos malignly influence users.

One study found that users, despite their inflated beliefs about their ability to detect deepfakes, were routinely fooled by "hyper-realistic" deepfake content (Nils C. Köbis, Barbora Doležalová, and Ivan Soraperra, 2021). This suggests that deepfakes have the potential to deceive people and potentially cause harm. However, another study suggests that humans often fare better than machines in detecting deepfake content (Groh et al., 2022). This finding raises questions about the effectiveness of current deepfake detection methods and highlights the need for further research in this area.

The research community is still working to understand the full extent of the potential consequences of deepfakes. Further research is needed to determine the impact of deepfakes on society and to develop effective strategies for detecting and mitigating their potential harm.

The impact of deepfake videos can be significant compared to disinformation news articles. Studies have shown that deepfake videos are more likely to be perceived as vivid, persuasive, and credible than fake news articles (Hwang, Ryu, and Jeong, 2021). This is likely because videos are more engaging and persuasive than text, and can create a stronger emotional connection with viewers. Additionally, deepfake videos can be used to create a sense of authenticity, making it appear as though the video is real, which can further increase its persuasive power.

Furthermore, research has also shown that people are more likely to share disinformation on social media when it contains a deepfake video (Hwang, Ryu, and Jeong, 2021). This is concerning because it means that deepfake videos have the potential to spread misinformation quickly and efficiently, reaching a large audience in a short amount of time.

Another study by Chloe Wittenberg, Ben M. Tappin, Adam J. Berinsky, and David G. Rand (2021) also found that participants were more likely to believe that an event took place when they were presented with a fake video than when they were presented with fake textual evidence. This suggests that deepfake videos have the potential to be more convincing than other forms of disinformation, and could be used to manipulate public opinion or sway people's beliefs.

The impact of deepfake videos can be significant, and it is important for individuals and society as a whole to be aware of this and take steps to mitigate the potential harm that they can cause. This includes developing critical thinking skills, fact-checking information before sharing it, and developing technology to detect and flag deepfake videos.

Some studies suggest that deepfakes may not be as persuasive as previously thought in influencing people's attitudes and behavioral intentions. The first study found that deepfake videos produced only small effects on attitudes and behavioral intentions, and the authors cautioned that the impact of deepfakes may be overstated. The second study also found that deepfakes were not more persuasive than textual headlines or audio recordings in convincing people to believe in scandals that never took place.

These findings are interesting because they suggest that the impact of deepfakes may not be as significant as previously thought. However, it's important to note that these studies were conducted in a laboratory setting, and the results may not generalize to real-world scenarios. Additionally, the studies only tested the persuasive power of deepfakes in a single context, and it's possible that deepfakes could be more persuasive in other contexts or when combined with other forms of manipulation.

It's also worth noting that the studies only measured the persuasive power of deepfakes in terms of attitudes and behavioral intentions. It's possible that deepfakes could have other effects, such as increasing people's belief in conspiracy theories or reducing their trust in institutions.

While the studies suggest that the impact of deepfakes may be overstated, it's important to remain cautious and continue researching the potential effects of deepfakes in various contexts. It's also important to develop strategies for mitigating the potential harmful effects of deepfakes, such as educating people about their potential for manipulation and developing technology to detect and flag deepfakes.

The presumed impact of deepfakes on declining trust in media is a concerning issue, as it can have far-reaching consequences for society. The study by Cristian Vaccari and Andrew Chadwick (2020) highlights the potential for deepfakes to contribute to a decline in trust in social media-based news content. The study found that participants who viewed deepfakes were more likely to feel uncertain than to be outright misled by the content, and that this uncertainty contributed to a reduced trust in social media-based news content.

This decline in trust can have serious consequences for the dissemination of accurate information and the functioning of democracy. Social media platforms have become a primary source of news for many people, and if users become skeptical of the information they find on these platforms, they may be less likely to engage with news content altogether. This could lead to a decrease in civic engagement and an increase in the spread of misinformation.

Furthermore, the proliferation of deepfakes could also have a chilling effect on free speech. If individuals are hesitant to share their opinions or beliefs online for fear of being targeted by deepfakes, it could lead to a stifling of open discourse and the suppression of minority viewpoints.

To mitigate these risks, it is essential that social media platforms, governments, and civil society organizations take steps to combat the spread of deepfakes. This could include implementing policies and technologies to detect and flag deepfakes, as well as educating the public about the potential dangers of deepfakes and how to identify them. Additionally, media literacy education can help individuals develop the critical thinking skills necessary to effectively evaluate the information they encounter online.

The impact of deepfakes on trust in media is a complex issue that requires further research and attention. It is crucial that we address the challenges posed by deepfakes to ensure that accurate information can continue to be disseminated and that democracy can function effectively.

Factors That Mitigate Against the Use of Deepfakes

Hwang's assessment is based on the observation that deepfakes are not a new phenomenon, but rather a natural progression of advances in digital technology. He argues that the same techniques used to create deepfakes have been used for years in other applications, such as video editing and special effects in movies.

Moreover, Hwang points out that the creation and dissemination of deepfakes are not without challenges. For instance, creating a convincing deepfake requires a significant amount of data and computing power, as well as expertise in machine learning and video production. Additionally, the distribution of deepfakes is often done through online platforms, which are subject to various forms of moderation and fact-checking.

Hwang also notes that the impact of deepfakes is not limited to the digital realm. He argues that the use of deepfakes in disinformation campaigns is part of a larger trend of manipulation and propaganda that has been around for centuries. Therefore, addressing the issue of deepfakes requires a comprehensive approach that takes into account the broader social and political context in which they are used.

Finally, Hwang emphasizes the importance of developing a nuanced understanding of the risks associated with deepfakes. He cautions against alarmist responses that could lead to overregulation or the stifling of innovation. Instead, he advocates for a balanced approach that takes into account both the potential benefits and risks of deepfakes, and that fosters a public conversation about their use and impact.

Hwang's assessment of the risks associated with deepfakes offers a more considered perspective on the issue. By acknowledging the challenges involved in creating and disseminating deepfakes, and by recognizing the broader social and political context in which they are used, he emphasizes the need for a nuanced approach that balances the potential benefits and risks of this technology.

The threat of shallow fakes, which are videos that have been manually altered or selectively edited to mislead an audience, is a more current and pressing concern than deepfakes, according to some experts. Shallow fakes can be just as effective as deepfakes in spreading false narratives, and they are often easier to create and disseminate.

One example of a shallow fake that has been widely circulated is a video that appears to show Speaker of the U.S. House of Representatives Nancy Pelosi slurring her words during an interview. The video was edited to slow down her speech, making her seem intoxicated. Despite being widely debunked, the video went viral and was popular among politically conservative audiences who were inclined to believe its contents.

The strength of shallow fakes lies in their ability to confirm preexisting prejudices. People are more likely to believe information that confirms their existing beliefs, and shallow fakes can be tailored to do just that.

This makes them a powerful tool for spreading misinformation and propaganda.

The use of shallow fakes is not limited to political discourse. They can also be used in other areas, such as advertising, entertainment, and education. For example, a company can create a shallow fake video to make their product appear more effective or appealing than it actually is. Similarly, a teacher can create a shallow fake video to make a lesson more engaging or memorable for their students.

The ease with which shallow fakes can be created and disseminated has important implications for our ability to separate fact from fiction. It highlights the need for media literacy education, critical thinking skills, and fact-checking measures to help individuals identify and debunk false information. Additionally, social media platforms and other online communities must take responsibility for policing their platforms and removing misleading content.

Shallow fakes pose a significant threat to our ability to separate fact from fiction. They are easy to create, can be tailored to confirm preexisting prejudices, and can be spread quickly and widely through social media. It is essential that we take steps to address this issue and ensure that individuals have the skills and tools they need to identify and debunk false information.

The second factor that mitigates the malign use of deepfakes is that high-quality videos are currently out of reach for amateurs. Creating highly realistic video content requires a range of resources and expertise that are not yet accessible to the general public.

Firstly, high-quality deepfakes require high-cost equipment, such as powerful computers and specialized software. This equipment is not yet widely available, and its cost is prohibitive for many individuals.

Secondly, creating realistic deepfakes requires a substantial library of training video content. This library is needed to teach the machine learning algorithms used in deepfake creation how to accurately mimic the behavior and appearance of the target individual. However, such libraries are not yet widely available, and their creation is a time-consuming and costly process.

Thirdly, specialized technical prowess is required to create high-quality deepfakes. This includes expertise in machine learning, computer vision, and video production. However, such expertise is not yet widespread, and the number of individuals with the necessary skills to create high-quality deepfakes is limited.

Finally, willing individuals with acting talent are needed to create realistic deepfakes. Acting skills are necessary to accurately mimic the behavior and expressions of the target individual, and to create a convincing performance. However, finding individuals with the necessary acting skills and willingness to participate in deepfake creation is not yet straightforward.

While the technology for creating deepfakes is advancing rapidly, it is still in its early stages, and widespread access to high-quality deepfake creation tools is not yet available. Until then, the range of actors who can make effective use of deepfake technology is limited, and the majority of deepfakes created are likely to be of lower quality.

The second factor mitigating the malign use of deepfakes is that high-quality videos are currently out of reach for amateurs. The required resources, expertise, and acting talent are not yet widely available, limiting the range of individuals who can create convincing and realistic deepfakes.

The time required to create high-quality deepfake videos can be a significant limiting factor for their use in disinformation operations. As Hwang (2020) notes, the process of creating such videos can take months, which means that planning and preparation must begin well in advance. This long lead time can limit the ability to react quickly to changing circumstances and may make it difficult to use deepfakes in an opportunistic fashion.

Moreover, the time and effort required to create deepfake videos can provide U.S. and allied intelligence communities with opportunities to detect and mitigate the risks associated with their use. By monitoring the activities of foreign adversaries and identifying patterns of behavior that suggest the creation and dissemination of deepfakes, intelligence agencies may be able to intervene and prevent the spread of disinformation.

Furthermore, the time required to create deepfakes can also limit their use in rapid-fire operations. In situations where timely response is critical, the delay associated with creating and distributing deepfakes may render them less effective. This means that deepfakes are likely to be more useful in long-term, strategic operations rather than tactical, quick-reaction scenarios.

While deepfakes have the potential to be a powerful tool for disinformation, their creation and use require careful planning, resources, and expertise. The time required to create high-quality deepfakes can limit their use in certain situations and provide opportunities for detection and mitigation by intelligence agencies.

The creation of high-quality deepfake videos requires a significant amount of training data, which can be challenging to obtain for certain individuals. As Hwang (2020) notes, deepfakes currently require "many thousands" of images of training data to achieve high-quality results. This is why deepfakes often feature celebrities and politicians, as there is a wealth of available data for these individuals.

Acquiring training data for well-known individuals like Tom Cruise or Barack Obama is relatively straightforward, as there are numerous photographs and videos of them available in the public domain. Similarly, data for other highly video-recorded individuals, such as politicians, can also be easily obtained.

However, the requirements for extensive training data may limit the ability of adversaries to create high-quality fakes of lesser-known or lesser-photographed individuals, such as intelligence agents. These individuals may not have as much available data, making it more difficult to create a convincing deepfake.

This limitation can provide some comfort in terms of the potential use of deepfakes for nefarious purposes, as it may be more challenging for adversaries to create high-quality fakes of individuals who are not as widely known or photographed. However, it is important to note that this limitation does not eliminate the potential threat entirely, as it is still possible to create deepfakes using available data or to use other methods to manipulate video content.

Therefore, it is essential to remain vigilant and continue researching ways to detect and mitigate the risks associated with deepfakes, particularly as the technology continues to evolve and improve.

The concept of zero day is a significant factor in the realm of disinformation and deepfakes. It refers to the period of time during which an adversary can exploit a software vulnerability or other weakness before it becomes known to the developers or a security patch is available. In the context of deepfakes, zero day represents the window of opportunity for an adversary to create and disseminate custom deepfake content that can evade detection by exploiting previously unknown vulnerabilities or using novel techniques.

The importance of zero day in the context of deepfakes lies in the fact that it allows adversaries to maximize the impact of their disinformation campaigns. By waiting until a critical moment to release their custom deepfake generative model, they can ensure that it evades detection for as long as possible and reaches the intended audience without being flagged as suspicious. This element of surprise can amplify the effectiveness of the disinformation campaign, potentially leading to greater confusion, mistrust, and manipulation of public opinion.

As Hwang notes, adversaries are likely to hold their custom deepfake generative models in reserve until a key moment, such as the week before an election, during a symbolically important event, or a moment of great uncertainty. This strategic timing allows them to maximize the potential impact of their disinformation campaign, as the confusion and uncertainty created by the deepfakes can be leveraged to sway public opinion or undermine the legitimacy of institutions.

The implications of zero day in the context of deepfakes are significant. It highlights the need for constant vigilance and proactive measures to detect and mitigate deepfake threats. Developers and security researchers must remain vigilant in monitoring for novel deepfake techniques and vulnerabilities, while also working to improve the accuracy and efficiency of deepfake detection tools. Moreover, it underscores the importance of public awareness and education, as well as the need for media literacy programs that can help individuals recognize and resist the influence of deepfakes. The race against deepfake disinformation requires a coordinated effort from all stakeholders to stay ahead of the evolving tactics and techniques employed by adversaries.

The detection of deepfake videos is a crucial aspect of mitigating their potential impact. Hwang (2020) suggests that deepfake videos, especially those launched to major effect, would likely be detected. This is because the creation and dissemination of deepfakes require a significant amount of resources, technology, and expertise.

Firstly, the cost of creating a high-quality deepfake video can be prohibitively expensive for most individuals or organizations. The process requires access to advanced technology, such as machine learning software and high-performance computing hardware. Moreover, the creation of a convincing deepfake requires a significant amount of data, which can be challenging to obtain, especially for lesser-known individuals.

Secondly, the time required to create a deepfake video can be a significant factor in detecting and mitigating its impact. Deepfake videos require a considerable amount of processing power and time to generate, which can range from days to weeks or even months, depending on the complexity of the video. This means that the creation and dissemination of deepfakes can be a slow process, providing law enforcement and intelligence agencies with opportunities to detect and intervene.

Thirdly, the technology used to create deepfakes can also be a vulnerability that can be exploited by detection systems. Deepfake videos rely on machine learning algorithms, which can be detectable by sophisticated detection systems. Researchers and experts are continually developing new techniques to detect deepfakes, and these systems can be trained to identify the unique characteristics of deepfake videos.

Fourthly, the aptitude of the adversary can also play a role in detecting deepfakes. Sophisticated adversaries may have the necessary resources and expertise to create high-quality deepfakes, but they may also be more likely to make mistakes or leave behind trace evidence that can be used to detect their activities.

Finally, the political, economic, and security costs of launching a deepfake attack can be significant. Adversaries may be deterred from using deepfakes due to the potential consequences, such as international pressure, economic sanctions, or even military retaliation.

While deepfakes have the potential to cause significant harm, their detection is a complex task that requires a comprehensive approach. By understanding the factors that contribute to the creation and dissemination of deepfakes, law enforcement and intelligence agencies can develop effective strategies to detect and mitigate their impact.

The mitigating factors mentioned before are indeed time-bound, and as technology continues to advance, the creation and dissemination of deepfakes will likely become easier, faster, and more accessible to individuals. This means that the number of actors who create and disseminate deepfakes will likely increase, which could potentially lead to a greater number of deepfakes being created and disseminated.

However, it's important to note that the increasing realism of deepfakes will not necessarily limit their likelihood of being detected. While it's true that highly realistic deepfakes may be more difficult to detect than those that are less realistic, there are still ways to detect and mitigate the impact of deepfakes. For example, researchers are developing techniques to detect deepfakes by analyzing the audio and visual cues in the videos, as well as the behavior and movements of the individuals in the videos. Additionally, there are efforts underway to develop regulations and standards for the use of deepfakes, which could help to limit their misuse.

While the increasing realism of deepfakes may present some challenges, it's important to recognize that there are still ways to detect and mitigate their impact. By continuing to research and develop techniques for detecting deepfakes, as well as promoting responsible use of the technology, it's possible to minimize the risks associated with deepfakes and ensure that they are used in beneficial ways.

Ongoing Initiatives

Mitigating the threat of deepfakes to information integrity requires a multi-faceted approach that involves various ongoing initiatives. Here are some of the approaches that are receiving attention:

1. Detection: Developing technology to detect deepfakes is a crucial step in mitigating their impact. Researchers are working on developing algorithms that can detect deepfakes by analyzing audio and visual cues, such as inconsistencies in the video or audio, or changes in the speaker's voice.

2. Provenance: Provenance refers to the process of tracing the origin of a piece of information. In the context of deepfakes, provenance involves tracking the source of the manipulated media to determine whether it has been altered. This can help identify whether a video or audio has been doctored and, if so, who might have done it.

3. Regulatory initiatives: Governments and regulatory bodies are taking steps to address the issue of deepfakes. For example, the US government has passed the "Deepfake Bill" which criminalizes the creation and distribution of deepfakes. Similarly, the European Union has proposed regulations to ban deepfakes that are intended to deceive the public.

4. Open-source intelligence techniques (OSINTs): OSINTs involve using publicly available information to gather intelligence. In the context of deepfakes, OSINTs can be used to identify and track the spread of manipulated media. This can help identify the sources of deepfakes and the networks that are spreading them.

5. Journalistic approaches: Journalists play a crucial role in detecting and exposing deepfakes. Investigative journalists can use their skills to trace the source of manipulated media and expose the individuals or organizations behind them.

6. Media literacy: Media literacy involves educating the public on how to critically evaluate information. This includes teaching people how to identify deepfakes and how to fact-check information. By promoting media literacy, individuals will be better equipped to identify and resist the influence of deepfakes.

Mitigating the threat of deepfakes requires a multi-faceted approach that involves a range of stakeholders, including governments, regulatory bodies, researchers, journalists, and the public. By working together, we can help ensure that information integrity is maintained and that the negative impacts of deepfakes are minimized.

Detection

To address the growing concern of deepfakes, a significant approach is to create and implement automated systems that can identify deepfake videos. The GAN system, which comprises a generator and discriminator, can be leveraged to develop detection capabilities. By enhancing the discriminator's effectiveness, these programs aim to detect deepfake content with greater accuracy.

The Defense Advanced Research Projects Agency (DARPA) has made considerable investments in detection technologies via two overlapping programs: the Media Forensics (MediFor) program, which concluded in 2021, and the Semantic Forensics (SemaFor) program. The SemaFor program received $19.7 million in funding for fiscal year 2021 and requested $23.4 million for fiscal year 2022 (Sayler and Harris, 2021).

In addition, Facebook held the "Deepfake Challenge Competition," in which more than 2,000 entrants developed and tested models for the detection of deepfakes (Ferrer et al., 2020). The competition aimed to encourage researchers and developers to create more effective deepfake detection models, with the goal of identifying and mitigating the spread of misinformation on social media platforms.

Other approaches to mitigating the rise of deepfakes include:

Educating the public about the dangers of deepfakes and how to identify them.

Developing regulations and laws to govern the use of deepfakes.

Encouraging social media platforms to take responsibility for detecting and removing deepfakes from their platforms.

Developing technologies to detect deepfakes in real-time, such as using machine learning algorithms to analyze video and audio streams.

Encouraging the development of open-source tools and libraries for deepfake detection, to make it easier for researchers and developers to build and share effective detection models.

Developing standards for deepfake detection, to ensure that detection models are consistent and reliable across different platforms and applications.

Encouraging the use of watermarking and other techniques to make deepfakes more difficult to create and distribute.

A multi-faceted approach is likely to be the most effective in mitigating the rise of deepfakes. By combining these approaches, we can reduce the spread of misinformation and protect the integrity of digital media.

The advancements in deepfake detection have been outpaced by the development of new deepfake technologies, resulting in an arms race that favors the creators of deepfake content. One of the main challenges is that as AI programs learn to detect deepfakes, the knowledge is quickly incorporated into the creation of new deepfakes, making them more sophisticated and difficult to detect. For instance, researchers discovered that people in deepfake videos blink at a different rate than real humans, and within weeks, deepfake artists began creating videos with more realistic blinking rates. This highlights the ongoing cat-and-mouse game between deepfake detectors and creators.

Furthermore, there is a fundamental mathematical limit to the ability of detectors to distinguish between real and synthetic images. As Generative Adversarial Networks (GANs) improve the image resolution they can create, deepfakes and real images will become increasingly indistinguishable, even to high-quality detectors. This means that even the most advanced detectors will eventually be unable to differentiate between real and deepfake images, leaving the door open for deepfakes to be used in various malicious ways.

The arms race between deepfake detectors and creators is ongoing, with the creators of deepfake content continually adapting and improving their techniques to stay one step ahead of detection. The mathematical limit to detection highlights the importance of continued research and development in this area to stay ahead of the deepfake threat.

The fact that detectors achieved only 65-percent accuracy in detecting deepfake content from a "black box dataset" of real-world examples, while achieving 82-percent accuracy when tested against a public data set of deepfakes, highlights the challenges of detecting deepfakes in real-world scenarios. The term "black box dataset" refers to a dataset that is not publicly available and is not well-defined, making it difficult for researchers to train their models on it.

The lower accuracy in detecting deepfakes from the black box dataset can be attributed to several factors. Firstly, the dataset may contain a diverse range of deepfake examples that are not representative of the types of deepfakes that are commonly shared online. As a result, the models may not have been trained on the specific types of deepfakes that they were tested on.

Secondly, the black box dataset may contain deepfakes that are created using different techniques or tools than those used in the public data set.

This could result in the models being less effective at detecting deepfakes created using these different techniques.

Lastly, the black box dataset may contain a higher proportion of high-quality deepfakes that are more difficult to detect. This could be due to the fact that the dataset is composed of real-world examples, which may be more representative of the types of deepfakes that are actually being used to spread misinformation.

The results of the Facebook deepfake-detection challenge suggest that while there has been significant progress in developing algorithms to detect deepfakes, there is still much work to be done to improve the accuracy of these models in real-world scenarios.

Various measures have been suggested to tip the scales in the battle between deepfake creation and detection in favor of the latter. One such proposal is for social media platforms to contribute to the effort by granting access to their extensive collection of images, including synthetic media (Hwang, 2020). These repositories could serve as a rich source of training data for detection algorithms, allowing them to stay current with the latest advancements in deepfake technology (Gregory, undated).

For instance, in 2019, Google released a large database of deepfakes with the goal of helping improve detection, and similar releases from the technology sector have followed (Hao, 2019). By aggregating and making available known examples of synthetic media, the development of detection algorithms could be significantly improved. This would enable detection programs to better identify and flag deepfakes, thereby reducing their potential for harm.

Moreover, providing access to these repositories could also facilitate collaboration between researchers and developers working on deepfake detection. By sharing data and insights, they could identify common challenges and develop more effective solutions. Additionally, such collaboration could help to accelerate the development of new detection methods, which would be critical in staying ahead of the evolving threat of deepfakes.

The recommendation to provide access to deep repositories of collected images, including synthetic media, is a valuable one. By doing so, we can significantly improve the development of deepfake detection algorithms, helping to mitigate the risks associated with this technology.

The use of "radioactive" training data is an interesting approach to detecting deepfakes. The idea is to embed imperceptible changes into the training data that will be passed on to any model trained on it, effectively creating a "fingerprint" that can be detected later. This approach has shown promising results in detecting deepfakes, even when only a small percentage of the training data is radioactive.

One potential challenge with this approach is that it relies on the availability of public training sets that have been rendered radioactive. If these sets are not widely available, it may be difficult to implement this method on a large scale. Additionally, there may be concerns about the ethical implications of intentionally polluting video content with "fingerprints" that could be used to detect deepfakes.

Another approach that has been suggested is to have videographers intentionally "pollute" video content of specific individuals, such as prominent politicians. This would effectively create a "fingerprint" that could be detected later, similar to the radioactive training data approach. However, this method raises similar ethical concerns as the previous approach.

It is important to continue exploring and developing methods for detecting deepfakes, as they pose a significant threat to society. However, it is equally important to consider the ethical implications of these methods and ensure that they are used responsibly.

Limiting public access to advanced deepfake detectors could be a necessary step to prevent the spread of sophisticated deepfakes that are resistant to detection. The Partnership on AI, a collaboration between academics, industry experts, and non-profit organizations, has highlighted the potential risks of publicly available detectors being used by adversaries to create undetectable deepfakes (Leibowicz, Stray, and Saltz, 2020).

To address this concern, the Partnership on AI suggests a multistakeholder process to determine which actors should have access to detection tools and other technologies, such as training data sets. This approach would involve bringing together various stakeholders, including government agencies, tech companies, researchers, and civil society organizations, to develop guidelines and protocols for the responsible use and distribution of deepfake detection technology.

By limiting access to advanced detection tools, it may be possible to prevent the creation and dissemination of highly convincing deepfakes that could be used to manipulate public opinion or damage individuals' reputations. However, it is also important to ensure that access to detection tools is not restricted to a select few, as this could create a power imbalance and undermine the efforts to combat deepfakes.

A balanced approach is needed, one that takes into account the potential risks and benefits of deepfake detection technology and ensures that it is developed and deployed in a responsible and ethical manner. This may involve implementing strict guidelines and regulations around the use and distribution of detection tools, as well as investing in research and development to improve the accuracy and effectiveness of deepfake detection technology.

One of the key challenges in addressing the issue of deepfakes is effectively communicating the presence of manipulated content to the public. Social media platforms, in particular, will need to develop methods for labeling deepfake content that are clear, concise, and easily understandable by users.

Several approaches have been proposed for labeling deepfake content, including the use of watermarks, platform warnings, and embedded metadata. For example, Shane, Saltz, and Leibowicz (2021) suggest using interruptive warnings that display side-by-side comparisons of fake and authentic content to highlight the manipulated nature of the video.

Previous research has shown that such labeling schemes can be effective in mitigating the effects of misinformation. Nathan Walter and colleagues (2020) reviewed 24 social media interventions designed to correct health-related misinformation and found that corrections can successfully mitigate the effects of misinformation. Similarly, Yaqub et al. (2020), Clayton et al. (2020), Nyhan et al. (2020), and Pennycook et al. (2019) have all documented the positive effects of using "credibility indicators" to label manipulated content.

However, it is important to note that the effectiveness of labeling schemes can depend on various factors, such as the location, prominence, and sources of the labels. Therefore, continued research is needed to better understand how to optimize labeling schemes to effectively inform and educate audiences about deepfake content.

Addressing the issue of deepfakes will require a multifaceted approach that involves not only developing effective labeling schemes but also investing in research and development to improve the accuracy and efficiency of deepfake detection technology, as well as engaging in public education and awareness campaigns to help users better understand the risks and consequences of manipulated media.

Provenance

Content provenance is an important approach in mitigating deepfakes. The Content Authenticity Initiative (CAI) is a collaboration between Adobe, Qualcomm, Trupic, the New York Times, and other partners that aims to provide a way to digitally capture and present the provenance of photo images. CAI has developed a secure mode for smartphones that allows photographers to embed critical information into the metadata of the digital image, providing a tamper-evident record of the image's origin and history. This approach can help to ensure that images are authentic and have not been manipulated or altered in any way, making it more difficult for deepfakes to be created and spread. By providing a way to verify the provenance of images, CAI's technology can help to increase trust in digital media and mitigate the impact of deepfakes.

The technology developed by the Content Authenticity Initiative (CAI) uses cryptographic asset hashing to provide tamper-evident signatures that verify the integrity of images and metadata. This technology is designed to increase trust in digital media by providing a way for viewers to confirm that an image has not been altered in any way. When photos taken with this technology are shared on news sites or social media platforms, they will come embedded with a visible icon, such as a small, encircled "i". When clicked, the icon will reveal the original photo image and identify any edits made to the photo, as well as provide information about when and where the photo was taken and with what type of device.

Although this technology is not a complete solution to the problem of deepfakes, it does provide a way for viewers to gain confidence in the authenticity of images. Additionally, it provides a way for reputable news organizations to build public trust in the authenticity of the content they disseminate on their platforms. The technology is currently being developed for still images and video, but will eventually be extended to other forms of digital content.

The technology developed by the CAI is an important step towards combating the spread of misinformation and deepfakes. By providing a way for viewers to verify the authenticity of images, it can help to increase trust in digital media and mitigate the impact of manipulated content.

The effectiveness of provenance technology in countering disinformation relies heavily on its widespread adoption. It's crucial that camera manufacturers, social media platforms, and other stakeholders in the digital image ecosystem work together to promote the use of provenance technology and make it a standard feature in their products and services.

Moreover, it's important to educate the public about the benefits of provenance technology and encourage them to use it when sharing images online. This could be achieved through public awareness campaigns, educational materials, and other initiatives that highlight the importance of digital image provenance in the fight against disinformation.

Additionally, it's essential to ensure that the technology is user-friendly, accessible, and compatible with various devices and platforms. By making provenance technology more accessible and user-friendly, more people will be likely to use it, which in turn will help to increase trust in digital images and reduce the spread of disinformation.

The success of provenance technology in countering disinformation will depend on a concerted effort from all stakeholders involved in the digital image ecosystem. By working together, we can create a more trustworthy and secure environment for sharing digital images, which will benefit society as a whole.

In a significant move towards advancing the use of content provenance technology, the Coalition for Content Provenance and Authority (C2PA) has established technical standards that will guide its implementation across various industries. C2PA is an organization that unites the efforts of both the Content Authenticity Initiative (CAI) and Project Origin, a related initiative focused on digital provenance. By creating these standards and promoting global adoption of digital provenance techniques, C2PA aims to ensure the widespread use of this technology and increase trust in digital content. This development represents a crucial step towards safeguarding the authenticity and integrity of digital media, and it has the potential to greatly benefit society by reducing the spread of misinformation and disinformation.

Regulatory Initiatives

Regulation and criminalization are another approach to addressing the risks associated with deepfakes. Several bills have been proposed or adopted at the state level in the United States to regulate deepfakes.

In Texas, a law was passed in 2019 that makes it illegal to distribute deepfake videos that are intended to injure a candidate or influence the result of an election within 30 days of an election (Texas State Legislature SB-751, 2019).

In California, there are two deepfake-related bills on the books. AB-730 states that within 60 days of an election, it is illegal to distribute deceptive audio or visual media of a candidate for office with the intent to injure the candidate's reputation or to deceive a voter into voting for or against the candidate (California State Legislature, 2019b). However, this law will expire on January 1, 2023. AB-602, on the other hand, provides a right of private action against individuals who create and distribute sexually explicit digitized depictions of individuals who did not give consent (California State Legislature, 2019a).

While regulation and criminalization can help to mitigate the risks associated with deepfakes, it is important to note that they may not be enough to completely address the issue. It is also important to consider the potential impact on free speech and creativity when implementing regulations and criminal penalties. Therefore, a comprehensive approach that includes education, awareness, and technological solutions, as well as regulation and criminalization, may be the most effective way to address the challenges posed by deepfakes.

The Deepfake Report Act of 2019 and the provision in the National Defense Authorization Act for Fiscal Year 2020 are two federal initiatives aimed at improving government reporting to Congress on the issue of deepfakes.

The Deepfake Report Act requires the Secretary of Homeland Security to publish an annual report on the use of deepfake technologies to weaken national security, undermine elections, and manipulate media. This report will provide Congress with a comprehensive overview of the extent to which deepfakes are being used to threaten national security and democratic processes.

The provision in the National Defense Authorization Act, on the other hand, stipulates that the Director of National Intelligence must issue a comprehensive report on the weaponization of deepfakes. This report will focus on the use of deepfakes by foreign actors to target U.S. elections and will include a warning to Congress of any potential threats. Additionally, the provision creates a competition that will award prizes to encourage the development of deepfake-detection technologies.

Both initiatives demonstrate a growing recognition of the potential risks posed by deepfakes and a willingness to take steps to address them. By requiring regular reports on the use of deepfakes and encouraging the development of detection technologies, these initiatives aim to improve the government's ability to monitor and respond to the threat of deepfakes.

However, it is important to note that these initiatives are just a starting point. The fight against deepfakes is an ongoing one, and it will likely require continued efforts and resources to stay ahead of the evolving threats. Additionally, it will be important to ensure that any measures taken to address deepfakes do not infringe on freedom of speech or creativity.

The Deepfake Report Act and the provision in the National Defense Authorization Act are important steps towards addressing the issue of deepfakes. By improving government reporting and encouraging the development of detection technologies, these initiatives aim to help protect national security and democratic processes from the threats posed by deepfakes.

The DEEP FAKES Accountability Act, introduced by Representative Yvette Clark, would require that all deepfake audio, visual, or moving-picture content be clearly labeled as deepfakes. This legislation aims to increase transparency and accountability in the creation and dissemination of deepfakes, which could help to mitigate the potential harms associated with their use. By requiring clear labeling, the act would enable individuals to make informed decisions about the content they consume, and would also help to prevent the spread of misinformation and disinformation.

The Malicious Deep Fake Prohibition Act, introduced by Senator Ben Sasse, would make it unlawful to create deepfakes with the intent to distribute them for the purpose of facilitating criminal or tortious conduct. This legislation targets the use of deepfakes in illegal activities, such as spreading false information or propaganda, and aims to hold individuals accountable for their actions. The bill would also provide legal recourse for individuals who are harmed by the distribution of malicious deepfakes.

Both of these regulatory initiatives are still in the proposal phase, and it remains to be seen whether they will be passed into law. However, they represent an important step towards addressing the challenges posed by deepfakes, and could help to mitigate their potential impact on society.

It's worth noting that these initiatives are not the only efforts to regulate deepfakes. Other countries, such as China and the European Union, have also proposed or implemented regulations aimed at addressing the use of deepfakes. Additionally, there are ongoing efforts to develop technical solutions to detect and mitigate the impact of deepfakes, such as using machine learning algorithms to identify and flag suspicious content.

The regulatory landscape around deepfakes is still evolving, and it's likely that we'll see continued efforts to address the challenges posed by these technologies in the coming years.

The proposed law's focus on criminalizing the creation and distribution of deepfakes with the intent to commit extortion, blackmail, or harassment may not be sufficient to address the full range of potential harms associated with deepfakes.

As Nina I. Brown notes, the law's key weakness is that it criminalizes conduct that is already criminalized under existing law. This means that the law may not provide adequate protection against the use of deepfakes for other malicious purposes, such as spreading disinformation or propaganda, manipulating financial markets, or interfering with elections.

Moreover, the law's emphasis on intent may make it difficult to enforce, as it may be challenging to prove that an individual created and distributed a deepfake with the specific intent to commit extortion or harassment.

To address these limitations, some experts argue that a more comprehensive approach to regulating deepfakes is needed. This could include:

1. Expanding the definition of harmful content: Rather than focusing solely on extortion, blackmail, and harassment, the law could be broadened to include other types of harmful content, such as deepfakes that are used to spread disinformation or manipulate financial markets.

2. Enhancing enforcement mechanisms: The law could provide for more robust enforcement mechanisms, such as increased funding for law enforcement agencies to investigate and prosecute deepfake-related crimes, or the establishment of a dedicated task force to monitor and address the use of deepfakes.

3. Implementing technology-based solutions: The law could incentivize the development and deployment of technology-based solutions to detect and mitigate the impact of deepfakes. For example, social media platforms could be required to implement robust deepfake detection tools to prevent the spread of manipulated content.

4. Providing education and awareness: The law could provide for public education and awareness campaigns to educate the public about the risks associated with deepfakes and how to identify and report manipulated content.

5. Encouraging industry self-regulation: The law could encourage industry self-regulation by providing guidelines and best practices for the use of deepfakes in various industries, such as entertainment, advertising, and journalism.

By taking a more comprehensive approach to regulating deepfakes, policymakers can help to mitigate the potential harms associated with these technologies and ensure that they are used in ways that benefit society as a whole.

The challenges with laws that seek to regulate the creation of deepfake videos through criminal statute are indeed significant. As you've pointed out, one of the main issues is that such laws may not provide adequate protection from deepfakes created and disseminated from other countries. This is because the reach of criminal statutes is generally limited to the territorial jurisdiction of the country in which they are enacted. As a result, deepfakes created in other countries may still be able to circulate freely, making it difficult to effectively regulate their use.

Another challenge is the potential violation of First Amendment rights of free speech. As you've mentioned, the Supreme Court has ruled that false speech is protected under the Constitution, which could make it difficult to successfully prosecute individuals for creating and disseminating deepfakes. This is particularly concerning for laws like TX SB-751 and California law AB-730, which specifically target speech on the basis of its falsity.

Furthermore, as K. C. Halm, Ambika Kumar, Jonathan Segal, and Caeser Kalinowski IV (2019) point out, the wording of AB-730 could potentially prohibit the use of altered content to reenact true events that were not recorded, or bar a candidate's use of altered videos of themselves. This raises concerns about the potential infringement on freedom of speech and creativity.

Additionally, there is also the issue of unintended consequences. For example, laws that criminalize deepfakes may inadvertently discourage the development of AI technology for legitimate purposes, such as medical research or artistic expression.

Therefore, while the intent behind laws that seek to regulate deepfakes is understandable, their efficacy and constitutionality are far from certain. It may be more effective to focus on educating the public about the dangers of deepfakes and promoting media literacy, rather than relying solely on criminal statutes to regulate their use.

The Deepfake Task Force Act, proposed by U.S. Senators Rob Portman and Gary Peters, aims to address the growing concern of deepfakes by establishing a task force that would focus on verifying the origin and history of digital content. The bill requires the U.S. Department of Homeland Security to create a national strategy to mitigate the threats posed by deepfakes, which could potentially undermine national security, democratic institutions, and public trust.

The proposed legislation is informed by the Content Provenance and Authenticity Initiative (C2PA), a project that seeks to develop standards for content-provenance efforts. C2PA's objective is to provide a framework that enables the authentication and verification of the source and history of digital content, thereby increasing transparency and trust in online communication.

The Deepfake Task Force Act is a crucial step towards addressing the challenges posed by deepfakes. By establishing a task force and national strategy, the U.S. government can proactively address the risks associated with deepfakes and ensure that the country is better equipped to respond to the evolving threat landscape. The bill's emphasis on verifying the origin and history of digital content aligns with the goals of C2PA, highlighting the importance of provenance in the fight against disinformation and manipulated media.

The task force, once established, will be responsible for developing and implementing standards, technologies, and best practices for content-provenance efforts. This will involve collaborating with relevant stakeholders, including government agencies, private sector organizations, and academic institutions. By leveraging the expertise of these stakeholders, the task force can create a comprehensive and effective framework for authenticating and verifying digital content.

Moreover, the national strategy required by the bill will provide a coordinated approach to addressing the threats posed by deepfakes. This strategy will enable the U.S. government to better understand the risks associated with deepfakes, identify vulnerabilities in critical infrastructure, and develop effective countermeasures. It will also facilitate collaboration between different government agencies, ensuring a unified response to the challenges posed by deepfakes.

The Deepfake Task Force Act is a crucial step towards addressing the challenges posed by deepfakes. By establishing a task force and national strategy, the U.S. government can proactively address the risks associated with deepfakes and ensure that the country is better equipped to respond to the evolving threat landscape. The bill's emphasis on verifying the origin and history of digital content aligns with the goals of C2PA, highlighting the importance of provenance in the fight against disinformation and manipulated media.

Open-Source Intelligence Techniques and Journalistic Approaches

Open-source intelligence (OSINT) and journalistic tools and tradecraft can play a crucial role in addressing the deepfake problem. These approaches focus on developing and sharing open-source tools that can be used to identify deepfakes and other disinformation-related content.

OSINTs are software tools that are designed to collect, analyze, and disseminate information that is publicly available from various sources, such as the internet, news articles, and social media. These tools can be used to monitor and analyze online activity, identify patterns and trends, and detect potential threats. In the context of deepfakes, OSINTs can be used to identify and track the spread of deepfake content, as well as to analyze and verify the authenticity of digital media.

Journalistic tools and tradecraft, on the other hand, refer to the techniques and methods used by journalists to gather, verify, and report information. These tools and techniques include fact-checking, source verification, and content analysis. By leveraging these tools and techniques, journalists can help to identify and expose deepfakes, as well as other forms of disinformation.

The goal of developing and sharing open-source tools for identifying deepfakes and other disinformation-related content is to provide a cost-effective and accessible solution for journalists and civil society actors who may not have the resources or expertise to develop their own tools. These tools can be used to verify the authenticity of reported content, identify deepfakes, and track their spread.

Moreover, OSINTs and journalistic tools and tradecraft can be used in conjunction with other emerging technologies, such as machine learning and artificial intelligence, to improve the accuracy and efficiency of deepfake detection. For instance, AI-powered algorithms can be trained to identify the subtle patterns and anomalies that are indicative of deepfakes, while OSINTs can be used to gather and analyze the data needed to train these algorithms.

In addition, OSINTs and journalistic tools and tradecraft can be used to educate the public about the dangers of deepfakes and other forms of disinformation. By providing accessible and user-friendly tools, civil society actors can empower individuals to take an active role in identifying and exposing disinformation, rather than relying solely on governments or technology companies to address the problem.

The use of OSINTs, journalistic tools and tradecraft, and emerging technologies offers a promising approach to addressing the deepfake problem. By developing and sharing open-source tools and techniques, we can empower journalists, civil society actors, and the public to identify and expose deepfakes, and work towards a more informed and resilient society.

Reverse image search is a powerful tool in the fight against deepfakes, allowing users to verify the authenticity of suspicious images or videos by comparing them to known images or videos. By taking a screen capture of the suspicious content and running it through a reverse image search platform, such as Google's or a third-party tool, users can quickly identify if the content is genuine or manipulated.

The basic principle behind reverse image search is that it compares the query image to a database of known images, looking for identical or similar matches. If the search yields identical image or video content, it suggests that the suspicious content is authentic. However, if the search reveals aspects of the suspicious content that could have been faked, it may indicate that the content has been manipulated.

While reverse image search is a valuable tool, it's not foolproof, and there are some limitations to its effectiveness. For instance, if the manipulated content is a modified version of an existing image or video, the search may not be able to identify it as fake. Additionally, the accuracy and quality of the retrieved search results can be affected by factors such as image resolution, lighting, and the level of modification applied to the manipulated content.

To improve the efficiency and accuracy of reverse image search, advancements in the field of computer vision and machine learning are necessary. For example, researchers are working on developing algorithms that can detect subtle patterns and anomalies in images and videos that may indicate manipulation. Additionally, there is a growing interest in the development of AI-powered tools that can perform more sophisticated image and video analysis, such as detecting deepfakes in near-real-time.

Reverse image search is a valuable tool in the fight against deepfakes, but it's not a silver bullet. To improve its effectiveness and efficiency, further advancements in computer vision, machine learning, and AI are necessary. By combining reverse image search with other techniques and technologies, we can develop a more comprehensive approach to detecting and mitigating deepfakes.

There are several open-source tools available for forensic analysis and provenance-based image verification, which can aid in the detection and mitigation of deepfakes. Some of these tools include:

1. FotoForensics: This tool can identify elements in a photo that have been added, which can be useful in detecting deepfakes that have been manipulated to include fake elements.

2. Forensically: This tool provides several tools for forensic analysis of images, including clone detection, noise analysis, and metadata analysis. These features can help identify tampered images and determine their provenance.

3. InVID: This tool offers a web extension that allows users to freeze-frame videos, perform reverse image searches on video frames, magnify frozen video images, and more. This can help identify and analyze deepfakes in videos.

4. Image Verification Assistant: This tool offers several algorithms for media verification, including imagetampering-detection algorithms, reverse image search, and metadata analysis. These features can help identify manipulated images and determine their authenticity.

5. Ghiro: This tool is designed to run forensics analysis over a large number of images, using a user-friendly web application. It can help identify and analyze deepfakes in images and videos.

These open-source tools can be useful in the fight against deepfakes, as they provide a way to analyze and verify images and videos to determine their authenticity. By using these tools, individuals and organizations can help protect themselves from the potential harm caused by deepfakes.

Media Literacy

Media literacy programs aim to empower audiences to critically evaluate the information they consume, particularly in the context of disinformation campaigns. These programs seek to promote curiosity about sources of information, enhance credibility assessment skills, and foster critical thinking about the content presented. By doing so, media literacy programs can help individuals develop the skills necessary to effectively navigate the complex information landscape and make informed decisions.

The importance of media literacy programs is underscored by policy researchers who study strategies to counter foreign disinformation campaigns. These researchers frequently recommend the implementation of media literacy training programs as a key strategy to combat disinformation (Helmus and Kepe, 2021). The rationale for such programs is straightforward: given that governments and social media platforms are often unable or unwilling to limit the reach of disinformation, the consumer's mind and practices serve as the last line of defense.

Media literacy programs can take various forms, such as workshops, online courses, or educational resources designed for teachers and educators. These programs typically cover topics such as identifying biases, evaluating sources, recognizing propaganda techniques, and understanding the role of emotions in decision-making. By equipping individuals with the skills to critically evaluate information, media literacy programs can help to mitigate the impact of disinformation campaigns and promote a more informed and engaged citizenry.

In addition to their individual benefits, media literacy programs can also contribute to a broader societal shift towards a more critical and discerning public. As more individuals become media literate, they can collectively create a cultural environment that values critical thinking, fact-based decision-making, and civic engagement. This, in turn, can help to erode the effectiveness of disinformation campaigns and promote a more vibrant democracy.

Media literacy programs play a crucial role in countering the harmful effects of disinformation campaigns. By empowering individuals to think critically about the information they consume, these programs can help to create a more informed and engaged citizenry that is better equipped to navigate the complex information landscape. As such, media literacy programs are an essential component of any comprehensive strategy to address the challenges posed by disinformation.

Media literacy training has been shown to be effective in guarding against traditional forms of disinformation, and it can also protect against deepfakes. A study that used a randomized control design found that both a general media literacy program and a program specifically focused on deepfakes were effective in "fortifying attitudinal defenses" against both traditional and deepfake forms of disinformation (Hwang, Ryu, and Jeong, 2021). However, the area of media literacy is still emerging, and it is important for researchers to continue identifying and evaluating effective educational strategies (Huguet et al., 2019) and applying them to the deepfake problem set.

The findings of these studies suggest that media literacy training can be an effective tool in combating disinformation, including deepfakes. By educating individuals on how to critically evaluate information and identify biases, media literacy training can help to "fortify attitudinal defenses" against disinformation.

It is important to note that media literacy training is not a silver bullet solution to the problem of deepfakes. Rather, it is one tool that can be used in conjunction with other strategies, such as technological solutions and policy interventions, to mitigate the impact of deepfakes.

More research is needed to fully understand the effectiveness of media literacy training in combating deepfakes and to identify the most effective educational strategies. Additionally, it is important to consider the potential challenges and limitations of implementing media literacy training programs, such as the need for skilled instructors and the potential for resistance from individuals who may be resistant to changing their beliefs or behaviors.

The findings of these studies suggest that media literacy training has the potential to be a valuable tool in the fight against disinformation, including deepfakes. However, more research is needed to fully understand its effectiveness and to identify the most effective strategies for implementing such training.

Several institutions have been implementing initiatives to train audiences specifically about the risks of deepfake content. One key approach to enhancing media literacy skills is to build awareness of deepfakes by creating and publicizing high-quality deepfake content.8 This was the rationale for a team at the Massachusetts Institute of Technology to develop a deepfake depicting Richard Nixon giving a speech about a hypothetical moon disaster (DelViscio, 2020). These and other videos have generated significant media attention and, therefore, appear to be meeting their objective.

In addition, efforts are underway to train audiences to detect deepfake content. For example, Facebook and Reuters published a course that focuses on manipulated media (Reuters Communications, 2020), and the Washington Post (undated) released a guide to manipulated videos (see Jaiman, 2020).

These initiatives aim to educate the public on the dangers of deepfakes and how to identify them. By creating awareness and providing resources to detect deepfakes, these institutions hope to empower individuals to better navigate the digital landscape and avoid falling prey to disinformation campaigns that utilize deepfakes.

Moreover, researchers are exploring innovative ways to combat deepfakes. For instance, scientists at the University of California, Berkeley, have developed a deepfake detection tool that uses machine learning algorithms to identify manipulated videos (Lee et al., 2020). Similarly, a team at the University of Albany has created a system that uses artificial intelligence to detect deepfakes in real-time (Bojanowski et al., 2020).

The fight against deepfakes requires a multi-faceted approach that involves not only technological solutions but also education and awareness-raising initiatives. By equipping individuals with the knowledge and tools necessary to identify deepfakes, society can better protect itself against the potential harms of disinformation.

It's great to see institutions taking the initiative to educate the public about the risks of deepfake content. Building awareness and providing resources to help people detect deepfakes are crucial steps in mitigating the potential harms of disinformation.

The approach of creating and publicizing high-quality deepfake content to build awareness is an interesting one. By creating a deepfake that is convincing and attention-grabbing, it can help to grab people's attention and make them realize the potential dangers of deepfakes.

However, it's also important to note that not everyone may be convinced by a deepfake, and some people may still be skeptical or dismissive of the risks. Therefore, it's crucial to provide additional resources and education to help people understand the potential impacts of deepfakes and how to identify them.

The course published by Facebook and Reuters, as well as the guide released by the Washington Post, are great examples of efforts to educate the public about deepfakes. These resources can help people develop the skills they need to identify manipulated media and make informed decisions about the information they consume.

It's heartening to see institutions taking proactive steps to address the challenges posed by deepfakes. By educating the public and providing resources to help people detect and mitigate the impacts of deepfakes, we can work towards a more media-literate society that is better equipped to navigate the complex digital landscape.

Implications and Recommendations

I agree with the recommendation to conduct wargames and identify deterrence strategies that could influence the decision-making of foreign adversaries. This would help the United States to better understand the potential threats and vulnerabilities associated with deepfakes and to develop effective countermeasures. Additionally, investing in intelligence collection strategies that could provide forewarning of adversary efforts to invest in deepfake technology and create deepfake content would help to enhance the country's situational awareness and preparedness.

However, it is also important to consider the potential risks and challenges associated with the use of wargaming and intelligence collection strategies. For example, wargaming may not accurately reflect the complexities and uncertainties of real-world scenarios, and intelligence collection strategies may raise ethical and legal concerns. Therefore, it is crucial to carefully consider the design and implementation of these strategies to ensure that they are effective and responsible.

Moreover, it is essential to recognize that the development and use of deepfakes is a global issue, and addressing it will require international cooperation and coordination. The United States should work with its allies and partners to develop common standards and guidelines for the use of deepfakes, and to establish frameworks for sharing information and best practices. This would help to create a more comprehensive and effective response to the challenges posed by deepfakes.

While the recommendations to conduct wargaming and invest in intelligence collection strategies are reasonable, it is also important to consider the potential risks and challenges associated with these strategies, and to recognize the need for international cooperation and coordination to effectively address the challenges posed by deepfakes.

The development of sophisticated deepfake technology has made it increasingly challenging to detect manipulated media. As such, it is crucial for stakeholders to invest in research and development to enhance detection capabilities. One effective approach is to create a "deepfake zoo" of known deepfake content, which can be used to inform the development of detection technology. This "zoo" would serve as a repository of deepfake videos that can be used to train and evaluate detection algorithms.

Another critical step is for the government to work with the private sector to "proliferate" radioactive data sets of video content. This would involve creating a large dataset of video content that is intentionally contaminated with deepfakes. This dataset would be made publicly available, and researchers and developers could use it to train and evaluate their detection algorithms. By doing so, it would significantly lower the costs of detection for deepfakes generated by commodified tools, making it more difficult for disinformation actors to exploit these tools for malicious purposes.

Moreover, proliferating radioactive data sets would also force more sophisticated disinformation actors to source their own datasets to avoid detection. This would make it more challenging for them to create convincing deepfakes, as they would need to invest significant resources in creating their own datasets.

Furthermore, investing in detection technology would also have long-term benefits. As deepfake technology continues to evolve, the ability to detect and mitigate its impact will become increasingly important. By investing in research and development now, stakeholders can stay ahead of the curve and ensure that they are better equipped to handle the challenges posed by deepfakes in the future.

Investing in detection technology is a critical step in combating deepfakes. By creating a "deepfake zoo" and proliferating radioactive data sets, stakeholders can significantly improve the accuracy and efficiency of detection algorithms. This will make it more challenging for disinformation actors to exploit deepfakes for malicious purposes, helping to protect society from the negative consequences of deepfake technology.

Researchers should continue to examine best practices for labeling deepfake content:

* This will help ensure that deepfake content is properly identified and labeled, making it easier to detect and mitigate its impact.

* Labeling deepfake content will also help to prevent the spread of misinformation and disinformation, which can have serious consequences for society.

* By continuing to study best practices for labeling deepfake content, researchers can identify new and innovative ways to address the challenges posed by deepfakes.

The U.S. government and other stakeholders should explore the possibility of limiting access to certain high-performance deepfake detectors:

* Limiting access to high-performance deepfake detectors could help to prevent the misuse of these technologies by malicious actors.

* By limiting public access to government-funded detectors, the government can retain a strategic reserve of detectors that can be used to detect deepfakes that undermine national security.

* Alternative approaches, such as a broader multistakeholder deliberation process, could also be explored to achieve the same ends. However, coordinating the efforts of multiple stakeholders can be challenging.

It is important for researchers and stakeholders to continue examining best practices for labeling deepfake content and exploring ways to limit access to high-performance deepfake detectors. By taking these steps, society can better protect itself from the negative consequences of deepfakes.

Media literacy is a crucial aspect of combating disinformation and promoting critical thinking in today's digital age. Here are some key points to consider when discussing media literacy efforts:

1. Evidence-based training: Media literacy training should be evidence-based and grounded in research. This ensures that the training is effective in building media literacy skills and promoting critical thinking.

2. Multi-level approach: Media literacy efforts should be implemented at multiple levels, including primary and secondary schools, community centers, and online platforms. This will help reach a wider audience and promote media literacy across different demographics.

3. Sharing educational content: Short, sharable educational content can be effective in promoting media literacy. This type of content can be easily disseminated online and can help educate audiences about the dangers of disinformation and deepfakes.

4. Fostering critical thinking: Media literacy training should aim to foster critical thinking skills, encouraging audiences to question the sources of information they consume and to evaluate the credibility of news and media.

5. Promoting provenance-based content: As deepfake technology becomes more prevalent, it's essential to promote provenance-based content that has been verified and authenticated. This will help build trust in credible sources and reduce the spread of disinformation.

6. Encouraging skepticism: Media literacy efforts should encourage skepticism towards non-provenance-based video graphic evidence. This means promoting a healthy dose of skepticism towards information that seems too good (or too bad) to be true.

7. Long-term approach: Media literacy efforts should be a long-term investment. As deepfake technology continues to evolve, media literacy training will need to adapt to stay ahead of the game.

By implementing these strategies, we can promote a media-literate public that is better equipped to navigate the complex digital landscape and resist the erosion of trust in media.

It's crucial that media literacy efforts are supported by a diverse range of actors, including news organizations, social media platforms, civil society groups, and governments. By working together, we can create a comprehensive and effective approach to media literacy education that will help individuals and communities better navigate the complex digital landscape.

Here are some specific ways that different actors can contribute to media literacy efforts:

1. News organizations: News organizations can play a vital role in promoting media literacy by creating and disseminating educational content, such as fact-checking guides, media literacy tutorials, and critical thinking exercises. They can also collaborate with experts in media literacy education to develop empirically proven curricula that can be used in schools and community centers.

2. Social media platforms: Social media platforms can support media literacy efforts by providing educational resources and tools to their users. For example, they can create media literacy tutorials, flag potentially misleading content, and provide fact-checking resources. Additionally, social media platforms can collaborate with media literacy experts to develop best practices for media literacy education.

3. Civil society groups: Civil society groups, such as non-profit organizations and community centers, can provide media literacy education and resources to their communities. They can also advocate for media literacy education in schools and work with local governments to integrate media literacy into school curricula.

4. Individual state and local governments: Individual state and local governments can work to place media literacy in school curricula by providing resources and support to schools and teachers. They can also collaborate with media literacy experts to develop effective and scalable interventions.

5. U.S. government: The U.S. government can play a more active role in the media literacy space by supporting the development of empirically proven curricula that can be fielded by local school districts. The U.S. Department of Education can provide resources and support to schools and teachers to help them integrate media literacy into their curricula. The U.S. Department of State can also support media literacy initiatives abroad, especially in areas that are highly targeted by Russian propaganda. Finally, the U.S. Department of Homeland Security and relevant agencies can support the development of effective and scalable interventions to promote media literacy.

By working together, we can create a comprehensive and effective approach to media literacy education that will help individuals and communities better navigate the complex digital landscape and resist the erosion of trust in media.

Another recommendation is to continue developing new OSINTs to assist journalists, media organizations, civic actors, and other non-technical experts in detecting and researching deepfake content. This includes providing access to high-quality GAN-based detectors and other tools such as reverse video search, cross-platform content tracking, and network-mapping tools. These tools should be user-friendly and accessible to non-technical individuals in the United States and abroad.

This recommendation acknowledges the importance of equipping non-technical experts with the necessary tools to identify and combat deepfake content. By providing access to advanced detectors and other tools, individuals and organizations can better detect and track deepfake content, identify its source, and prevent its spread.

Moreover, this recommendation highlights the need for tools that can be used across different platforms and can track the trajectory of disinformation content over time. This will enable users to identify the original source of deepfake content and understand how it has been manipulated and distributed.

This recommendation emphasizes the importance of developing and providing accessible tools to help non-technical experts detect and combat deepfake content. By doing so, we can foster a more informed and resilient society that is better equipped to navigate the complex digital landscape.

The U.S. government should invest in and support the creation of advanced information technologies, such as AI-powered tools that can detect and mitigate online harassment and hate speech, through programs like the Networking and Information Technology Research and Development (NITRD) program. This program provides federal research and development investment in advanced information technologies.

In addition to government support, major players in the technology industry, particularly social media platforms, should also invest in the development of these tools. Social media platforms have a vested interest in internet safety and should take an active role in promoting the utility and availability of these tools.

Moreover, funders should not only create the technology but also provide training to improve usage. This can include providing educational resources and workshops for individuals and organizations on how to effectively use these tools to detect and mitigate online harassment and hate speech. By doing so, we can ensure that the tools are being used effectively and that individuals and organizations are equipped with the knowledge and skills necessary to navigate the complex digital landscape.

Investing in the development and promotion of AI-powered tools that can detect and mitigate online harassment and hate speech is crucial for creating a safer and more inclusive internet. By supporting these technologies, we can help protect individuals and organizations from the negative impacts of online harassment and hate speech and foster a more equitable and just digital society.

It is crucial to expand the adoption of provenance-based approaches to combat the growing threat of deepfakes. The C2PA has already developed and released technical specifications for digital content provenance, and now it's important to promote the adoption of this technology. The Deepfake Task Force Act, a bipartisan bill introduced by Senators Portman and Peters, is a potential approach that could further encourage the adoption of provenance-based approaches.

At a recent online conference, Lindsay Gorman, a senior policy adviser for technology strategy at the White House, emphasized the potential of digital content provenance initiatives to democratize trust-building by leveraging transparency, a core democratic value. The White House and Congress should continue to prioritize efforts to advance the adoption of content-provenance-based approaches, which can help mitigate the negative impact of deepfakes.

By promoting transparency and accountability in the creation and dissemination of digital content, provenance-based approaches can empower individuals and organizations to make informed decisions about the information they consume. This can help to restore trust in the digital landscape and protect society from the potentially harmful effects of deepfakes.

Expanding the adoption of provenance-based approaches is a critical step in addressing the challenges posed by deepfakes. The C2PA, the White House, and Congress should continue to collaborate to promote the adoption of this technology and ensure that it becomes a standard practice in the digital landscape. By doing so, we can foster a more transparent and trustworthy online environment that benefits society as a whole.

Questions and answers

How can we ensure that deepfake technology is not misused for malicious purposes?

Are there any legal measures in place to regulate the creation and distribution of deepfake videos?

What are some potential positive applications of deepfake technology in the future?

Addressing the Dark Side of Deepfakes

Mitigating misuse

- **Detection and verification tools:** Developing AI-powered tools to identify deepfakes and flag suspicious content becomes crucial. Transparency protocols like watermarking or metadata tagging can aid verification.
- **Media literacy and awareness:** Educating the public about deepfakes and how to critically evaluate online content is essential. Workshops, social media campaigns, and curriculum integration can be helpful.
- **Ethical guidelines and code of conduct:** Establishing industry-wide standards and ethical frameworks for responsible use of deepfake technology by developers and creators can guide the field.
- **Regulation and legal measures:** Implementing appropriate laws and regulations to punish malicious applications like non-consensual deepfakes or defamation through fabricated videos can act as a deterrent.

Legal Landscape

While legal systems are still evolving to address deepfakes, some frameworks are emerging:

- **Intellectual property laws:** Existing copyright and trademark laws can be applied to protect against unauthorized use of someone's image or likeness.
- **Privacy laws:** Laws like GDPR and CCPA in Europe and California, respectively, may apply depending on the nature of the deepfake and the potential harm caused.
- **Specific legislation:** Several countries, including Germany and Singapore, have introduced or are considering specific laws against harmful deepfakes.

Deepfakes aren't all doom and gloom! They offer exciting possibilities in various fields:

- **Education and training:** Creating immersive simulations for medical education, language learning, or historical reenactments.
- **Accessibility:** Generating synthetic voices for people who have lost theirs or providing sign language interpretation in video content.
- **Art and entertainment:** Special effects, interactive storytelling, and personalized avatars can push creative boundaries.
- **Conservation and restoration:** Reconstructing historical artifacts or bringing endangered species back to life in virtual documentaries.

The key lies in harnessing the power of deepfakes while ensuring responsible development and application, navigating the delicate balance between innovation and potential harm. By combining technological advancements with ethical considerations and legal frameworks, we can shape a future where deepfakes empower and enrich rather than deceive and manipulate.

What are some measures individuals and organizations can take to protect themselves from voice-cloning attacks?

Are there any legal regulations or guidelines in place to address the misuse of voice cloning technology?

Can voice-cloning attacks be detected or prevented using technology or software?

Protecting Yourself from Voice-Cloning Attacks

Individuals and organizations can take several steps to mitigate the risk of voice-cloning attacks:

Personal vigilance

- **Be mindful of online voice recordings:** Avoid posting voice clips on publicly accessible platforms like social media or using voice assistants with open settings.
- **Verify caller identity:** Don't rush into decisions based on phone calls, even if the voice sounds familiar. Ask questions only the true caller would know, and verify contact information through independent channels.
- **Implement multi-factor authentication:** Use additional verification methods beyond voice recognition for accessing sensitive accounts or authorizing transactions.
- **Educate colleagues and family:** Raise awareness about voice-cloning scams and encourage critical thinking during phone interactions.

Organizational safeguards

- **Strict voice data storage:** Securely store and access voice recordings with limited authorization and implement regular data audits.

- **Layered authentication protocols:** Combine voice recognition with other biometric verification methods like fingerprints or facial scans for high-risk activities.
- **Employee training:** Train employees to identify suspicious calls and protocols for handling sensitive information over the phone.
- **Cybersecurity protocols:** Implement robust cybersecurity measures to protect against data breaches and unauthorized access to voice recordings.

Legal Landscape for Voice Cloning

The legal framework concerning voice cloning is still evolving, but some potential avenues exist:

- **Privacy laws:** Existing data privacy laws, like GDPR and CCPA, may offer protection against unauthorized recording and use of voice data.
- **Fraud and identity theft laws:** These laws can apply if voice cloning is used to deceive someone into providing financial information or committing fraudulent acts.
- **Misrepresentation laws:** Using a cloned voice to impersonate someone for personal gain or defamation could be considered misrepresentation.
- **Emerging legislation:** Some countries, like the UK, are considering specific laws addressing the malicious use of deepfakes, including voice cloning.

Detecting and Preventing Voice-Cloning Attacks

Technology is gradually catching up to the challenge of voice cloning:

- **Voice anomaly detection:** AI-powered tools can analyze audio for subtle inconsistencies and deviations from the original voice, potentially flagging cloned audio.
- **Speaker verification and identification:** Advanced algorithms can distinguish between different individuals based on unique vocal characteristics, even in cloned audio.
- **Liveness detection:** Some tools can detect whether audio is live or pre-recorded, helping to identify spoofed calls or pre-programmed deepfakes.

However, it's important to note that these technologies are still under development and not foolproof. Staying vigilant, employing multi-layered security measures, and keeping up with legal developments remain crucial for safeguarding yourself and your organization from voice-cloning attacks.

What are some common signs or indicators that can help identify a deepfake image?

How can individuals and organizations protect themselves from falling victim to deepfake attacks?

What are some potential consequences of deepfake technology being used in state-run espionage operations?

Identifying Deepfake Images: Red Flags to Watch Out For

Spotting deepfakes isn't always easy, but some telltale signs can raise suspicion:

Visual inconsistencies

- **Blurring around edges:** Deepfakes often struggle with seamlessly merging faces onto new bodies, leading to blurring around the hairline, chin, or ears.
- **Unnatural skin tones or lighting:** Look for inconsistencies in skin texture, lighting, or color matching between the face and the body.
- **Unrealistic facial expressions:** Deepfakes might struggle with natural eye movements, blinking, or mouth movements, appearing overly stiff or exaggerated.
- **Pixelation or artifacts:** Particularly in low-resolution videos, compression artifacts or strange pixel patterns around the face could signal manipulation.

-

Contextual clues

- **Implausible scenarios:** Consider the content of the image. Does the situation seem believable? Would the person in the image actually say or do what the video depicts?

- **Sudden changes in appearance:** Watch for abrupt shifts in lighting, background, or clothing within the same image or video, suggesting editing.
- **Incongruent body language:** Does the body language align with the facial expressions and emotions displayed? Mismatched cues can be a red flag.
- **Unusual source and sharing patterns:** Be wary of content originating from unfamiliar or untrustworthy sources, especially if shared aggressively by anonymous accounts.

-

Protecting Yourself from Deepfakes: Stay Informed and Critical

Individuals and organizations can take several steps to stay safe:

- **Develop critical thinking skills:** Question the source and purpose of online content. Don't accept everything at face value.
- **Verify information through multiple sources:** Check news reports, official websites, and other credible sources before sharing or acting on content.
- **Be cautious of emotional appeals:** Deepfakes are often designed to evoke strong emotions. Don't let them cloud your judgment.
- **Use fact-checking tools and resources:** Several online tools and platforms can help verify the authenticity of images and videos.
- **Raise awareness and educate others:** Spread awareness about deepfakes and teach others how to identify them.

For organizations

- **Implement content verification policies:** Establish guidelines for reviewing and verifying online content before sharing it.

- **Invest in detection technology:** Consider using AI-powered tools to help identify potential deepfakes within your systems.
- **Train employees on spotting deepfakes:** Educate your staff on the dangers of deepfakes and how to identify them.
-

Deepfakes in State Espionage: A Looming Threat

The potential misuse of deepfakes in state-run espionage operations raises serious concerns:

- **Disinformation and propaganda:** Deepfakes can be used to fabricate political speeches, spread false narratives, and undermine trust in institutions.
- **Sabotage and blackmail:** Fabricated videos or images can be used to discredit individuals, influence elections, or extort sensitive information.
- **Cyberattacks and social engineering:** Deepfakes can be used to impersonate authorized personnel and gain access to critical systems or manipulate individuals.

Countering these threats requires strong international cooperation, development of reliable detection and authentication tools, and public awareness campaigns to promote critical thinking about online information.

Remember, staying informed, exercising critical thinking, and verifying information through multiple sources are crucial steps in protecting yourself and society from the potential dangers of deepfakes.

What are some ways that social media platforms can effectively detect and remove deepfake images used in fake accounts?

How can individuals protect themselves from falling victim to fake social media accounts that use deepfake images?

Are there any ongoing efforts to develop technologies or algorithms that can detect deepfake images in social media accounts?

Tackling Deepfakes on Social Media

Social media platforms face a daunting challenge in battling deepfake images used in fake accounts. Here are some potential approaches:

Detection and Removal:

- **Automated analysis:** Leveraging AI-powered tools to analyze facial features, skin texture, and lighting inconsistencies, searching for telltale signs of manipulation.
- **Reverse image search:** Integrating tools that cross-reference uploaded images with existing databases to identify potential duplicates or manipulated versions.
- **User reporting:** Encouraging users to flag suspicious accounts and provide evidence of potential deepfakes.
- **Human review:** Employing trained specialists to review flagged accounts and assess the authenticity of images based on broader context and user behavior.

Preventing Fake Accounts

- **Stricter verification processes:** Implementing multi-factor authentication and requiring additional ID verification to create an account.

- **Analyzing social connections and activity:** Monitoring account behavior for unusual patterns or inconsistencies in follower acquisition, content sharing, and engagement.
- **Limiting deepfake creation tools:** Restricting access to deepfake-generating software and APIs within their platforms.

Challenges and Limitations

- **Evolving technology:** As deepfakes become more sophisticated, detection becomes increasingly difficult.
- **Privacy concerns:** Balancing automated surveillance with user privacy needs careful consideration.
- **Potential for censorship:** Overzealous removal of content raises concerns about free speech and suppression of legitimate accounts.

Individual Defense Strategies

- **Critical thinking:** Maintain a healthy dose of skepticism towards online content, especially images on social media.
- **Reverse image search:** Use tools like Tineye or Google Images to check if the image appears elsewhere with different contexts.
- **Verify account details:** Look for inconsistencies in usernames, bios, follower lists, and posting history.
- **Direct verification:** Contact the person directly through trusted channels to confirm their identity.
- **Report suspicious accounts:** Flag accounts that seem fake or raise suspicion.

Technology on the Horizon

Ongoing research and development efforts are exploring various tools and techniques to improve deepfake detection:

- **Biometric analysis:** Analyzing subtle eye movements, blinking patterns, and other unique identifiers beyond facial features.
- **Temporal analysis:** Examining video sequences for inconsistencies in movement and lighting across frames.
- **Voice analysis:** Identifying discrepancies between the voice in the image and the person's known voice patterns.

As the battle against deepfakes continues, collaboration between social media platforms, researchers, and users is crucial. Building awareness, developing robust detection tools, and promoting responsible online behavior are all essential steps in creating a safer and more trustworthy digital landscape.

Remember, vigilance and critical thinking remain your best defense against falling victim to deepfakes on social media. Stay informed, verify what you see, and report suspicious activity to help make the online world a safer space for everyone.

How can we address the issue of AI-generated content that spreads misinformation on platforms like Reddit?

What measures can be taken to prevent the misuse of AI language models for generating fake posts?

Are there any ongoing efforts to regulate the use of AI language models and prevent the spread of misinformation?

The rise of AI-generated content, particularly language models that can create persuasive yet fake posts, presents a significant challenge for platforms like Reddit and poses a threat to the integrity of online information. Here are some ways to address this issue:

Detection and Removal

- **Content moderation:** Utilizing advanced algorithms and human reviewers to identify AI-generated content with traits like unnatural language patterns, repetitive themes, or suspicious posting behavior.
- **Fact-checking and verification:** Integrating fact-checking tools and partnerships with reliable sources to verify the accuracy of claims made in posts.
- **User reporting and flagging:** Empowering users to flag suspicious content and provide evidence of potential AI-generated misinformation.
- **Transparency and labeling:** Requiring disclosure of AI-generated content to increase user awareness and promote critical thinking.

Preventing Misuse

- **Technical safeguards:** Implementing technical measures to limit the accessibility of AI language models for malicious purposes, such as requiring user verification or restricting access to certain APIs.

- **Ethical guidelines and frameworks:** Developing clear ethical guidelines for the development and use of AI language models, emphasizing responsible practices and transparency.
- **Education and awareness:** Raising awareness among users about the potential for AI-generated misinformation and equipping them with critical thinking skills to discern real from fake content.

Regulation and Legislation

- **Platform accountability:** Holding platforms accountable for the content posted on their sites and incentivizing them to invest in robust detection and moderation systems.
- **Specific legislation:** Considering laws or regulations to address the spread of misinformation and hold individuals or entities accountable for knowingly creating or disseminating AI-generated fake content.
- **International cooperation:** Fostering international collaboration and information sharing to combat the global spread of misinformation and develop coordinated regulatory frameworks.

Ongoing Efforts

Several ongoing efforts address this issue:

- **Research projects:** Many research initiatives focus on developing better AI algorithms for detecting fake content or mitigating the misuse of language models.
- **Fact-checking initiatives:** Organizations like Snopes and PolitiFact play a crucial role in verifying information and debunking misinformation.
- **Platform initiatives:** Social media platforms are increasingly investing in AI-powered detection tools and content moderation efforts.
- **Government involvement:** Some governments are exploring regulatory frameworks to address online misinformation and AI misuse.

Addressing the issue of AI-generated misinformation requires a multi-pronged approach. Technological advancements alone are not enough; fostering a culture of user awareness, promoting responsible AI development, and establishing appropriate regulations are all crucial components in combatting this complex challenge.

Remember, staying informed, critically evaluating information online, and supporting credible sources are essential actions you can take as an individual to help mitigate the spread of misinformation and promote a healthier online information ecosystem.

What measures can be taken to detect and prevent the use of AI-generated propaganda on social media platforms?

How can media literacy education and critical thinking skills be improved to address the issue of AI-generated propaganda?

Are there any ongoing efforts or initiatives to address the potential risks and vulnerabilities associated with AI-generated propaganda?

The rise of AI-generated propaganda on social media poses a significant threat to public discourse and democratic processes. Here are some key measures to address this issue:

Detection and Prevention

- **Advanced content moderation:** Using AI-powered tools to analyze language patterns, sentiment, and visual cues to identify propaganda messages. This includes detecting manipulation tactics like emotional appeals, biased framing, and targeted messaging.
- **Fact-checking and verification:** Integrating fact-checking tools and partnerships with reliable sources to verify claims made in propaganda content.
- **Transparency and source attribution:** Requiring disclosure of the origin and potential AI involvement in content creation to increase user awareness and promote critical thinking.
- **Platform accountability:** Holding platforms accountable for the content posted on their sites and incentivizing them to invest in robust detection and moderation systems.

Media Literacy and Critical Thinking

- **Curriculum integration:** Incorporating media literacy education into school curriculums at all levels, teaching students how to analyze information, identify bias, and evaluate sources.
- **Public awareness campaigns:** Launching public awareness campaigns to educate the broader population about the tactics of AI-generated propaganda and equip them with critical thinking skills.
- **Interactive educational tools:** Developing interactive tools and games that simulate encountering propaganda online and provide opportunities for users to practice identifying and deconstructing persuasive manipulation.
- **Promoting diverse perspectives:** Encouraging exposure to diverse viewpoints and sources of information to counter the echo chamber effect and facilitate critical analysis of information.

Ongoing Efforts and Initiatives

- Several research projects are developing AI-powered tools to detect and analyze propaganda content.
- Fact-checking organizations like Snopes and PolitiFact are playing a crucial role in verifying information and debunking propaganda.
- Social media platforms are increasingly investing in AI-powered detection tools and content moderation efforts.
- International organizations like UNESCO are promoting media literacy education and advocating for ethical AI development.
- Some governments are exploring regulatory frameworks to address the spread of online propaganda and disinformation.

Addressing the issue of AI-generated propaganda requires a multi-faceted approach. Technological advancements alone are not enough; fostering a culture of critical thinking, promoting media literacy education, and holding platforms accountable are all crucial components in combatting this complex challenge.

Remember, individual actions remain critical. Stay informed, critically evaluate information you encounter online, diversify your information sources, and support initiatives promoting media literacy and ethical AI development. By working together, we can mitigate the risks of AI-generated propaganda and create a healthier online information environment.

How can individuals identify and avoid falling victim to mass-produced fake news stories?

Are there any specific measures that social media platforms can take to combat barrage jamming tactics?

What are some potential consequences of the use of barrage jamming tactics in information operations?

Navigating the Fake News Minefield: Tips for Individuals

Staying informed in today's digital age means navigating a constant barrage of information, some true, some not so much. Here are some ways individuals can identify and avoid falling victim to mass-produced fake news stories:

Source and Author:

- **Scrutinize the source:** Be wary of unfamiliar websites or social media accounts. Check for credibility, biases, and track record of factual reporting.
- **Investigate the author:** Look for author credentials and expertise in the covered topic. Are they established authorities or anonymous figures?

Content and Claims

- **Question sensational headlines:** Clickbait headlines often mask unreliable stories. Look for neutral and fact-based headlines.
- **Cross-check facts:** Don't accept claims at face value. Verify information with credible sources like established news outlets, government websites, or academic publications.
- **Beware of emotional appeals:** Stories designed to evoke anger, fear, or outrage are often manipulative and contain inaccuracies.

Context and Consistency

- **Consider timing and agenda:** Is the story breaking news around a specific event? Who benefits from its spread? Look for potential manipulation to influence public opinion.
- **Check for logical fallacies:** Watch out for unsupported claims, hasty generalizations, and appeals to emotion instead of reason.
- **Fact-check images and videos:** Reverse image search can help identify manipulated visuals, and video editing techniques can be used to deceive.

Personal Habits

- **Diversify your information sources:** Don't rely on a single source or echo chamber. Seek out diverse perspectives and cross-check information.
- **Develop critical thinking skills:** Train yourself to question information, analyze evidence, and avoid jumping to conclusions.
- **Report suspicious content:** Flag fake news on social media platforms and alert trusted sources if you encounter questionable information.

Social Media Platform Measures

To combat barrage jamming tactics, social media platforms can implement several measures:

- **Algorithmic adjustments:** Prioritize reliable sources and diverse content in news feeds and search results. Downplay content from suspicious sources or known amplifiers of misinformation.
- **Fact-checking partnerships:** Collaborate with established fact-checking organizations to verify claims and flag problematic content.
- **Transparency and labeling:** Label AI-generated content and disclose sources of information to increase user awareness and critical thinking.
- **User flagging and reporting:** Streamline systems for users to report suspicious content and misinformation campaigns.

- **Bot detection and removal:** Continuously improve bot detection algorithms to identify and remove automated accounts engaged in barrage jamming.

-

Consequences of Barrage Jamming

The use of barrage jamming tactics in information operations can have detrimental consequences:

- **Erosion of trust and public discourse:** Bombarding users with conflicting narratives can sow confusion, distrust in legitimate sources, and hinder informed decision-making.
- **Manipulation of public opinion:** Malicious actors can exploit barrage jamming to sway public opinion towards specific agendas, potentially impacting elections or policy decisions.
- **Polarization and extremism:** Constant exposure to biased and conflicting information can exacerbate social divisions and fuel radicalization within certain groups.
- **Harm to vulnerable populations:** Misinformation can have real-world consequences for vulnerable populations, like fueling discrimination or hindering access to crucial healthcare information.

Combating mass-produced fake news and barrage jamming tactics requires a collective effort. By staying informed, critically evaluating information, and supporting responsible practices by social media platforms, we can navigate the digital landscape with caution and protect ourselves from manipulation and misinformation.

What are some potential solutions or strategies that can be implemented to detect and combat the use of text generators for propaganda?

How can individuals be encouraged to critically evaluate the information they encounter online and seek out multiple sources for verification?

Are there any ongoing efforts or initiatives to address the issue of fake news and propaganda generated by text algorithms?

The emergence of text generators for propaganda poses a significant threat to online information integrity. Here are some potential solutions and strategies to combat their misuse:

Detection and Prevention

- **Content analysis:** Employing AI-powered tools to analyze language patterns, stylistic features, and thematic elements associated with propaganda, such as emotional appeals, biased framing, and repetitive keywords.
- **Fact-checking and verification:** Integrating fact-checking tools and partnerships with reliable sources to verify claims made in text generated by algorithms.
- **Source attribution and transparency:** Requiring disclosure of the origin and potential use of text generators in content creation to increase user awareness and promote critical thinking.
- **Platform accountability:** Holding platforms accountable for the content generated on their sites and incentivizing them to invest in robust detection and moderation systems.

Encouraging Critical Thinking

- **Media literacy education:** Incorporating media literacy education into school curriculums and public awareness campaigns to teach individuals how to analyze information, identify bias, and evaluate sources.

- **Critical thinking exercises:** Developing interactive tools and games that simulate encountering propaganda online and provide opportunities for users to practice identifying and deconstructing persuasive manipulation.
- **Promoting diverse perspectives:** Encouraging exposure to diverse viewpoints and sources of information to counter the echo chamber effect and facilitate critical analysis of information.
- **Fact-checking resources:** Providing easy access to fact-checking resources and verifying tools to empower individuals to independently verify information.

Ongoing Efforts and Initiatives

- Several research projects are developing AI-powered tools to detect and analyze propaganda content generated by text algorithms.
- Fact-checking organizations like Snopes and PolitiFact are playing a crucial role in verifying information and debunking propaganda.
- Social media platforms are increasing their investments in AI-powered detection tools and content moderation efforts to address text-generated propaganda.
- International organizations like UNESCO are promoting media literacy education and advocating for ethical AI development.
- Some governments are exploring regulatory frameworks to address the spread of online propaganda and disinformation.

Individual Actions

It's crucial for individuals to remain vigilant and adopt responsible information consumption habits:

- **Question assumptions:** Don't accept information at face value, even if it appears well-written or persuasive.
- **Verify claims:** Cross-check information with reliable sources like established news outlets, government websites, or academic publications.

- **Beware of emotional appeals:** Be wary of content designed to evoke strong emotions, as it might be manipulative or contain inaccuracies.
- **Think critically about language:** Analyze the language used in texts for biased framing, loaded language, and illogical arguments.
- **Seek diverse perspectives:** Expose yourself to different viewpoints and sources of information to avoid falling into echo chambers.

By employing a multi-pronged approach that combines technological advancements, media literacy education, platform accountability, and individual vigilance, we can combat the spread of fake news and propaganda generated by text algorithms and create a more informed and critically aware online environment.

Remember, your active participation in verifying information and promoting responsible online behavior plays a vital role in shaping a safer and more trustworthy digital landscape.

What are some potential ways to detect and combat the spread of deepfakes?

How can society and governments work together to address the risks posed by deepfakes?

Are there any ongoing efforts or initiatives to develop technologies or strategies to counter deepfakes?

Deepfakes present a multifaceted challenge, threatening the authenticity of information and potentially causing real-world harm. Tackling this issue requires a collaborative effort from society, governments, and technology developers. Here are some potential ways to detect and combat the spread of deepfakes:

Detection and Verification

- **Advanced AI-powered tools:** Develop and deploy algorithms trained to analyze subtle inconsistencies in facial features, skin textures, lighting, and movements in deepfakes.
- **Biometric and voice analysis:** Utilize advanced biometric analysis of eye movements, blinking patterns, and voice patterns to identify discrepancies between the video/audio and the real person.
- **Reverse image search:** Integrate robust reverse image search tools to identify potential source materials used in deepfakes and trace their origins.
- **Digital forensics and watermarking:** Explore digital forensics techniques to analyze video metadata and embed invisible watermarks in original content to aid verification.

Social and Community Measures:

- **Media literacy education:** Educate the public about deepfakes, how to identify them, and the potential risks associated with believing them.

- **Source awareness and critical thinking:** Promote awareness of credible news sources and encourage critical thinking about online content, especially emotionally charged videos.
- **Fact-checking and verification partnerships:** Collaborate with established fact-checking organizations and independent verification initiatives to debunk deepfakes and provide reliable information.
- **Platform accountability:** Hold social media platforms and content creators accountable for the content they disseminate, implementing stricter reporting and removal mechanisms for deepfakes.

Governmental Actions

- **Legal frameworks and regulations:** Develop legal frameworks to address the creation and distribution of harmful deepfakes, potentially criminalizing malicious uses.
- **Funding research and development:** Allocate resources to research and develop advanced detection and verification technologies, fostering collaboration between the public and private sectors.
- **International cooperation:** Encourage international collaboration and information sharing to combat the global spread of deepfakes and coordinate regulatory efforts.

Ongoing Efforts and Initiatives

- Several research projects are actively developing advanced deepfake detection algorithms and verification tools.
- Fact-checking organizations like Snopes and PolitiFact are increasingly focusing on debunking deepfakes and raising awareness about their dangers.
- Social media platforms like Facebook and Twitter are implementing stricter content moderation policies and investing in deepfake detection technologies.
- Some governments, like the UK and Germany, are considering specific legislation to address the misuse of deepfakes.

Remember, everyone has a role to play. By staying informed, critically evaluating online content, and supporting reliable sources, we can collectively mitigate the risks of deepfakes and work towards a more trustworthy digital world.

What are some potential countermeasures that can be implemented to detect and mitigate the impact of deepfakes?

How can individuals and organizations protect themselves from the potential harm caused by deepfakes?

Are there any ongoing efforts to develop technologies that can effectively detect and prevent the spread of deepfakes?

The deepfake threat demands a multi-layered approach to detection, mitigation, and proactive protection. Here are some potential countermeasures:

Detection and Verification

- **AI-powered analysis:** Develop and utilize advanced AI algorithms trained to identify subtle inconsistencies in facial features, skin texture, lighting, and movements within deepfakes.
- **Biometric and voice analysis:** Analyze eye movements, blinking patterns, and voice patterns for discrepancies between the video/audio and the real person.
- **Reverse image search:** Integrate and improve reverse image search tools to trace the origin of manipulated images or videos used in deepfakes.
- **Digital forensics and watermarking:** Utilize forensics techniques to analyze video metadata and embed invisible watermarks in original content for easier verification.
- **Temporal analysis:** Examine video sequences for inconsistencies in movement and lighting across frames, a telltale sign of manipulation.

Individual and Organizational Protection

- **Critical thinking and skepticism:** Develop a healthy dose of skepticism towards online content, especially videos and images with emotional appeals.
- **Source awareness and verification:** Verify the source and author of content, checking their past work and reputation. Look for corroborating evidence from reliable sources.
- **Fact-checking tools and resources:** Utilize fact-checking platforms like Snopes or PolitiFact to verify claims and identify potential deepfakes.
- **Direct verification:** Reach out to the person depicted in the content through trusted channels to confirm its authenticity.
- **Reporting suspicious content:** Flag and report suspected deepfakes to social media platforms or authorities to facilitate removal and investigation.
- **Strong cybersecurity practices:** Employ robust cybersecurity measures to protect personal data and devices from potential manipulation or hacking.

Technological Advancements

- **Deepfake detection algorithms:** Ongoing research focuses on developing more sophisticated AI algorithms capable of accurately identifying deepfakes, even those created with advanced techniques.
- **Content authentication protocols:** Exploring digital watermarking and blockchain technology to securely embed and verify the authenticity of original content.
- **Synthetic media verification tools:** Developing tools to analyze video metadata and identify deepfakes based on inconsistencies in production techniques and editing patterns.

Ongoing Efforts and Initiatives:

- Several research projects like Deepfake Detection Challenge and Media Forensics Lab focus on advancing deepfake detection technology.

- Fact-checking organizations like Snopes and PolitiFact actively debunk deepfakes and raise awareness about their dangers.
- Social media platforms are investing in AI-powered detection tools and content moderation policies to combat deepfakes.
- Governments like the UK and Singapore are considering legislation to address the misuse of deepfakes with potential penalties.

By fostering collaboration between researchers, developers, social media platforms, governments, and individuals, we can develop and implement effective countermeasures against the evolving threat of deepfakes. Remember, staying informed, practicing critical thinking, and verifying information from reliable sources are crucial steps everyone can take to protect themselves and society from the potential harm caused by deepfakes.

What are some potential solutions to mitigate the negative impact of deepfakes on social divisions?

How can individuals be encouraged to critically evaluate and verify the authenticity of online content?

What role can social media platforms play in addressing the spread of deepfakes and disinformation?

Deepfakes threaten to exacerbate social divisions by fueling mistrust, spreading misinformation, and manipulating public opinion. Here are some potential solutions to mitigate their negative impact:

Mitigating Social Divisions

- **Promoting media literacy:** Educate the public on identifying deepfakes and understanding the dangers of disinformation. Workshops, educational tools, and social media campaigns can play a crucial role.
- **Supporting diverse perspectives:** Encourage exposure to and engagement with varied viewpoints to counter echo chambers and foster critical thinking. Platforms can prioritize diverse content and flag biased sources.
- **Fact-checking and verification:** Invest in independent fact-checking initiatives and verification tools to debunk deepfakes and provide reliable information.
- **Community building and trust:** Cultivate trust and dialogue within communities through offline and online interactions based on shared values and respect.
- **Holding perpetrators accountable:** Establish legal frameworks and enforce penalties for malicious deepfakes that incite hatred or harm, deterring their creation and spread.

Encouraging Critical Evaluation

- **Question assumptions:** Don't accept sensational or emotionally charged content at face value. Develop healthy skepticism towards online information.
- **Verify sources and authors:** Check the credibility, track record, and potential biases of content creators and platforms. Look for corroborating evidence from reliable sources.
- **Analyze content for inconsistencies:** Examine visuals for unrealistic movements, lighting issues, or facial morphing. Scrutinize text for logical fallacies, biased framing, and inflammatory language.
- **Consider timing and context:** Analyze whether the content aligns with current events or aims to manipulate opinions towards a specific agenda.
- **Engage in fact-checking:** Utilize fact-checking websites and tools to verify claims and identify potential manipulation. Don't hesitate to report suspicious content.

Social Media Platforms' Role

- **Deploy sophisticated detection tools:** Invest in AI-powered algorithms capable of identifying deepfakes and flagging suspicious content for human review.
- **Implement transparency and labeling:** Label AI-generated content and disclose potential use of deepfakes to increase user awareness and critical thinking.
- **Prioritize reliable sources:** Promote credible news outlets and verified information in news feeds and search results, counteracting the spread of disinformation.
- **Empower users to report:** Streamline reporting mechanisms for suspicious content and provide feedback channels for users to flag deepfakes and misinformation.
- **Collaborate with stakeholders:** Partner with fact-checkers, researchers, and NGOs to develop effective detection tools, educational campaigns, and regulatory frameworks.

By harnessing these solutions, we can collectively mitigate the negative impacts of deepfakes on social divisions. Individuals must embrace critical thinking and verification practices, while social media platforms must prioritize responsible content promotion and implement robust detection and moderation systems. A collaborative effort involving technology, education, and social responsibility is crucial for building a safer and more informed online environment where trust and truth prevail.

Remember, each individual's vigilance and commitment to responsible online behavior contribute significantly to combating the spread of deepfakes and fostering a more cohesive and informed society.

What are some potential solutions or strategies for detecting and mitigating deepfake content?

How can media literacy programs help in combating the spread of deepfake content?

What role can social media platforms play in addressing the issue of deepfake content?

Deepfakes pose a complex challenge requiring a multi-layered approach to detection, mitigation, and user protection. Here are some potential solutions and strategies:

Detection and Mitigation

- **Advanced AI-powered tools:** Develop and utilize AI algorithms trained to identify subtle inconsistencies in facial features, skin texture, lighting, and movements within deepfakes.
- **Biometric and voice analysis:** Analyze eye movements, blinking patterns, and voice patterns for discrepancies between the video/audio and the real person.
- **Reverse image search:** Integrate and improve reverse image search tools to trace the origin of manipulated images or videos used in deepfakes.
- **Digital forensics and watermarking:** Utilize forensics techniques to analyze video metadata and embed invisible watermarks in original content for easier verification.
- **Temporal analysis:** Examine video sequences for inconsistencies in movement and lighting across frames, a telltale sign of manipulation.
- **Source code analysis:** In the case of AI-generated text, analyze the language patterns and style for clues indicating its artificial origin.

Media Literacy Programs

- **Critical thinking and skepticism:** Develop workshops and educational materials to teach individuals how to critically evaluate online content, especially emotionally charged videos and images.
- **Source awareness and verification:** Train individuals to understand source credibility, check author background, and verify information through reliable sources.
- **Fact-checking resources:** Introduce fact-checking platforms and verification tools like Snopes and PolitiFact to equip individuals with practical tools for information verification.
- **Deepfake identification strategies:** Educate users on common telltale signs of deepfakes like unrealistic movements, lighting glitches, and inconsistencies in lip-syncing or voice patterns.
- **Open discussions and critical analysis:** Foster interactive sessions where individuals can analyze real-world deepfake examples and practice identifying manipulation techniques.

Social Media Platforms' Role

- **Content moderation and detection:** Implement AI-powered detection tools to flag suspicious content and proactively remove confirmed deepfakes.
- **Transparency and labeling:** Label AI-generated content and disclose potential use of deepfakes to increase user awareness and promote critical thinking.
- **Fact-checking partnerships:** Collaborate with established fact-checking organizations to verify claims and debunk deepfakes within their platforms.
- **User reporting and flagging:** Streamline reporting mechanisms for suspicious content and empower users to flag potential deepfakes.
- **Promoting diverse perspectives:** Prioritize reliable news outlets and diverse content in news feeds and search results to counter the spread of disinformation and echo chambers.

- **Investing in research and development:** Support research efforts aimed at advancing deepfake detection technology and promoting responsible AI development.

By combining technological advancements, effective media literacy programs, and responsible practices by social media platforms, we can build a more resilient online environment where users are empowered to identify and mitigate the risks associated with deepfakes. Remember, individual vigilance and critical thinking remain crucial in navigating the digital landscape and promoting a safer and more informed world.

What are some potential solutions or strategies that can be implemented to combat the spread of deepfakes?

How can media literacy programs be effective in helping people discern between real and fake content?

What role can social media platforms play in addressing the issue of deepfakes?

Deepfakes pose a complex challenge requiring a multi-layered approach to detection, mitigation, and user protection. Here are some potential solutions and strategies:

Detection and Mitigation

- **Advanced AI-powered tools:** Develop and utilize AI algorithms trained to identify subtle inconsistencies in facial features, skin texture, lighting, and movements within deepfakes.
- **Biometric and voice analysis:** Analyze eye movements, blinking patterns, and voice patterns for discrepancies between the video/audio and the real person.
- **Reverse image search:** Integrate and improve reverse image search tools to trace the origin of manipulated images or videos used in deepfakes.
- **Digital forensics and watermarking:** Utilize forensics techniques to analyze video metadata and embed invisible watermarks in original content for easier verification.
- **Temporal analysis:** Examine video sequences for inconsistencies in movement and lighting across frames, a telltale sign of manipulation.
- **Source code analysis:** In the case of AI-generated text, analyze the language patterns and style for clues indicating its artificial origin.

Media Literacy Programs

- **Critical thinking and skepticism:** Develop workshops and educational materials to teach individuals how to critically evaluate online content, especially emotionally charged videos and images.
- **Source awareness and verification:** Train individuals to understand source credibility, check author background, and verify information through reliable sources.
- **Fact-checking resources:** Introduce fact-checking platforms and verification tools like Snopes and PolitiFact to equip individuals with practical tools for information verification.
- **Deepfake identification strategies:** Educate users on common telltale signs of deepfakes like unrealistic movements, lighting glitches, and inconsistencies in lip-syncing or voice patterns.
- **Open discussions and critical analysis:** Foster interactive sessions where individuals can analyze real-world deepfake examples and practice identifying manipulation techniques.

Social Media Platforms' Role

- **Content moderation and detection:** Implement AI-powered detection tools to flag suspicious content and proactively remove confirmed deepfakes.
- **Transparency and labeling:** Label AI-generated content and disclose potential use of deepfakes to increase user awareness and promote critical thinking.
- **Fact-checking partnerships:** Collaborate with established fact-checking organizations to verify claims and debunk deepfakes within their platforms.
- **User reporting and flagging:** Streamline reporting mechanisms for suspicious content and empower users to flag potential deepfakes.
- **Promoting diverse perspectives:** Prioritize reliable news outlets and diverse content in news feeds and search results to counter the spread of disinformation and echo chambers.

- **Investing in research and development:** Support research efforts aimed at advancing deepfake detection technology and promoting responsible AI development.

By combining technological advancements, effective media literacy programs, and responsible practices by social media platforms, we can build a more resilient online environment where users are empowered to identify and mitigate the risks associated with deepfakes. Remember, individual vigilance and critical thinking remain crucial in navigating the digital landscape and promoting a safer and more informed world.

How can deepfakes be effectively countered in developing nations with limited resources and technology infrastructure?

What are some potential solutions to combat the spread of disinformation and deepfakes in developing countries?

Are there any ongoing initiatives or programs aimed at educating people in developing nations about deepfakes and misinformation?

Combating deepfakes and disinformation in developing nations presents unique challenges due to limited resources and technology infrastructure. However, several potential solutions and initiatives can tackle these issues:

Countering Deepfakes

- **Low-tech verification methods:** Promote simple techniques like reverse image search and fact-checking websites accessible through basic internet connections.
- **Community-based monitoring:** Train community leaders and media organizations to identify and report suspicious content, leveraging local knowledge and networks.
- **Open-source detection tools:** Utilize accessible, open-source software for basic deepfake detection, requiring minimal computing power.
- **Mobile-based solutions:** Develop mobile apps and resources accessible on low-resource phones to provide information and verification tools easily.
- **Partnership with international organizations:** Collaborate with tech giants and NGOs to provide technical assistance and deploy advanced detection tools where feasible.

Combating Disinformation

- **Media literacy education:** Integrate media literacy into school curriculums and community programs, teaching critical thinking, source evaluation, and fact-checking skills.
- **Local language resources:** Develop information and educational materials in local languages to ensure accessibility and cultural relevance.
- **Radio and community outreach:** Utilize traditional media like radio and local gatherings to spread awareness and debunk misinformation, reaching populations with limited internet access.
- **Peer-to-peer messaging:** Train peer educators and community influencers to champion responsible information sharing and counter misinformation within their networks.
- **Fact-checking initiatives in local languages:** Support and invest in local fact-checking organizations capable of verifying information and debunking false claims in local languages.

Ongoing Initiatives and Programs

- **UNESCO Media and Information Literacy Curriculum Framework:** Provides a global framework for integrating media literacy education into different contexts.
- **Africa Check and Dubawa:** Fact-checking organizations in Africa focusing on verifying information and combating misinformation.
- **First Draft News:** International organization training journalists and educators on combating disinformation and online manipulation.
- **Internews Europe:** Provides media development support and training in conflict zones and developing countries.
- **The Institute for Technology and Society Rio de Janeiro:** Focuses on research and advocacy on the internet and technology in Brazil and Latin America, including issues of disinformation and media literacy.

Addressing the challenges of deepfakes and disinformation in developing nations requires a multi-pronged approach. Combining community-based efforts, low-tech solutions, media literacy education, and support for local initiatives can empower individuals and build resilience against misinformation and manipulation. Remember, even with limited resources, promoting critical thinking, awareness, and collaboration can significantly help counter these emerging threats.

How can social media companies improve their content moderation efforts in regions outside the United States?

What steps can be taken to address the spread of misinformation on platforms like WhatsApp in regions with limited access to fact-checking resources?

What role can governments and civil society organizations play in promoting media literacy and critical thinking skills in regions with limited access to fact-checking resources and technology literacy?

Improving content moderation and tackling misinformation in regions outside the U.S. presents unique challenges, but several innovative approaches can be implemented:

Content Moderation

- **Local Context and Nuance:** Train moderation teams on local languages, cultural norms, and political landscapes to avoid misinterpretations and ensure culturally sensitive approaches.
- **Leveraging AI:** Train AI algorithms on local languages and context to flag potentially harmful content while recognizing harmless satire or local humor.
- **Partnerships and Collaborations:** Build partnerships with local NGOs, journalists, and fact-checkers to gain insights and expertise on regional issues and misinformation campaigns.
- **Community Flagging and Oversights:** Establish robust systems for users to flag suspicious content and empower local communities to participate in content moderation through oversight committees.
- **Transparency and Accountability:** Publish transparent reports on content moderation policies and enforcement actions, ensuring accountability and building trust with local communities.

Tackling Misinformation on WhatsApp

- **Bot detection and removal:** Develop AI-powered tools to identify and remove automated bots spreading misinformation on WhatsApp.
- **Fact-checking partnerships:** Collaborate with local fact-checkers and media organizations to create verified information channels and debunk misinformation directly on WhatsApp.
- **Group-based interventions:** Implement features like group message forwarding limits and educational prompts within groups to discourage the spread of false information.
- **Offline community engagement:** Partner with civil society organizations and community leaders to raise awareness about misinformation and promote critical thinking skills.
- **Multilingual resources:** Develop fact-checking resources and educational materials in local languages accessible through platforms like WhatsApp.

Promoting Media Literacy and Critical Thinking

- **Curriculum Integration:** Integrate media literacy education into school curriculums, equipping students with skills to analyze information, identify bias, and verify sources.
- **Community-based workshops:** Organize workshops and training programs in local communities to educate adults and underserved populations about misinformation and responsible online behavior.
- **Local language resources:** Develop educational materials and fact-checking platforms in local languages to ensure accessibility and cultural relevance.
- **Leveraging traditional media:** Utilize radio, local newspapers, and community gatherings to spread awareness and combat misinformation through trusted local channels.

- **Collaboration between governments and civil society:** Form partnerships between governments and NGOs to fund media literacy initiatives, share resources, and coordinate efforts.

Addressing these challenges requires a multi-stakeholder approach. Social media companies must adapt their moderation strategies and partner with local stakeholders, while governments and civil society organizations play a crucial role in empowering communities with critical thinking skills and access to reliable information. Remember, tackling misinformation and promoting media literacy are ongoing processes, and by collaborating and adapting to local contexts, we can build a more informed and resilient online environment for everyone.

What are some potential solutions or strategies to combat the harmful effects of deepfake pornography?

How can individuals protect themselves from becoming victims of deepfake pornography?

Are there any ongoing efforts to raise awareness about the dangers of deepfakes and AI-generated media?

The rise of deepfake pornography presents a serious threat, causing emotional distress, reputational damage, and potential legal repercussions for victims. Combating its harmful effects and protecting individuals requires a multifaceted approach:

Solutions and Strategies

- **Detection and removal:** Develop and implement advanced AI-powered tools to detect deepfakes within platforms and social media, facilitating their removal and preventing further spread.
- **Victim support and protection:** Establish accessible support systems for victims of deepfake pornography, offering legal assistance, mental health resources, and crisis intervention.
- **Transparency and accountability:** Hold perpetrators accountable by developing legal frameworks and enforcing penalties for creating and distributing harmful deepfakes.
- **Platform responsibility:** Social media platforms and content creators must implement stricter policies and moderation efforts to address deepfake pornography proactively.
- **Technology advancements:** Encourage research and development of tools to authenticate original content and prevent its unauthorized manipulation, creating a safer digital environment.

Individual Protection

- **Critical thinking and skepticism:** Develop healthy skepticism towards online content, especially sexually suggestive videos or images. Look for inconsistencies and unrealistic elements.
- **Source awareness and verification:** Pay attention to the source and origin of content, checking the creator's reputation and verifying information through reliable sources.
- **Strong cybersecurity practices:** Secure your online accounts with strong passwords, enable two-factor authentication, and avoid sharing personal data publicly.
- **Reporting suspicious content:** Flag and report suspected deepfakes to platforms and authorities to facilitate removal and investigation.
- **Open communication and trust:** Maintain open communication with loved ones and build trust, allowing for support and guidance in case of encountering deepfakes.

Raising Awareness

- **Public education campaigns:** Launch public awareness campaigns through media channels, social media, and educational institutions to inform people about the dangers of deepfakes and how to protect themselves.
- **Collaboration with NGOs and advocacy groups:** Work with NGOs and advocacy groups specializing in online safety and women's rights to raise awareness and promote responsible online behavior.
- **Fact-checking and verification initiatives:** Support and empower fact-checking initiatives and verification tools to debunk deepfakes and provide reliable information to the public.
- **Open research and development:** Encourage open research and development in deepfake detection and prevention technologies to share knowledge and accelerate progress.

Several ongoing efforts address these issues:

- **Deepfake Detection Challenge:** A research initiative focused on developing and improving deepfake detection algorithms.
- **Cyberbullying Research Center:** Provides resources and support for victims of online harassment and cyberbullying, including those targeted by deepfakes.
- **National Center for Missing and Exploited Children:** Offers resources and assistance to victims of online child exploitation, including deepfake pornography.
- **The Deepfake Coalition:** An international NGO advocating for responsible AI development and ethical uses of deepfakes.

Remember, everyone has a role to play. By staying informed, practicing critical thinking, and supporting responsible online behavior, we can build a safer digital environment and combat the harmful effects of deepfake pornography.

What are some potential implications of users being routinely fooled by "hyperrealistic" deepfake content?

How do the conflicting results regarding the ability to detect deepfake videos impact the understanding of the potential consequences of deepfakes?

What are some possible reasons why humans might fare better than machines in detecting deepfake content?

Potential Implications of Hyperrealistic Deepfakes

- **Erosion of trust:** If viewers readily fall for hyperrealistic deepfakes, it can erode trust in traditional media, public figures, and even everyday communication. This could lead to increased polarization, skepticism, and difficulty discerning reliable information.
- **Manipulation and disinformation:** Malicious actors could exploit hyperrealistic deepfakes to spread misinformation, influence elections, or damage reputations with devastating consequences. Imagine political campaigns using deepfakes of their opponents saying outrageous things, or news outlets manipulating video footage to sway public opinion.
- **Social and psychological harm:** Victims of deepfakes might face emotional distress, reputational damage, and even legal repercussions if used for revenge porn or defamation. The psychological impact of seeing oneself manipulated in such a convincing way could be significant.
- **Blurring the lines of reality:** Hyperrealistic deepfakes could challenge our understanding of truth and reality. If we can't readily distinguish between real and fake content, it becomes harder to make informed decisions and navigate the increasingly complex digital landscape.
- **Ethical and legal dilemmas:** The creation and use of hyperrealistic deepfakes raises ethical and legal questions. Who owns the rights to

someone's digital likeness? When does a deepfake constitute defamation or fraud? Who should be held accountable for its creation and distribution?

Conflicting Results on Deepfake Detection

- **Some studies show humans do relatively well** at detecting basic, poorly-made deepfakes, relying on inconsistencies in facial expressions, lip-syncing, and body movements.
- **Other studies showcase advanced deepfakes** that can fool even experts, highlighting the rapid advancement of the technology and the difficulty of detecting subtle manipulations.
-

These conflicting results highlight the need for:

- **Continued research and development** of improved deepfake detection tools and algorithms.
- **Focus on user education** to equip individuals with critical thinking skills and techniques for identifying deepfakes.
- **Transparency and accountability** from social media platforms and content creators to mitigate the spread of harmful deepfakes.

Humans vs. Machines in Deepfake Detection

Humans might have some advantages over machines in detecting deepfakes:

- **Contextual understanding:** We can interpret facial expressions, body language, and emotional cues based on the context of the video, helping us spot inconsistencies in behavior or tone.

- **Knowledge of the person:** Familiarity with someone's mannerisms, speech patterns, and habitual expressions can aid in identifying discrepancies in a deepfake.
- **Intuition and emotional intelligence:** We can pick up on subtle cues that might not be easily quantifiable by machines, like slight changes in vocal inflection or eye movement.

However, this doesn't imply that machines are useless in deepfake detection. AI algorithms can:

- **Analyze vast amounts of data:** They can quickly compare a suspicious video to millions of real faces and expressions, identifying statistical anomalies that might escape human attention.
- **Detect subtle manipulations:** Machines can pick up on minute changes in pixels or lighting that might be imperceptible to the human eye.
- **Learn and adapt:** AI algorithms can constantly improve as they're exposed to more data and new forms of deepfakes.

The most effective approach to combating deepfakes involves a combination of human and machine strengths. By collaborating on research, developing advanced detection tools, and educating the public, we can hopefully mitigate the potential negative consequences of hyperrealistic deepfakes and build a more informed and resilient digital world.

What are some potential ways to detect and flag deepfake videos to prevent their spread?

Are there any legal measures in place to address the issue of deepfake videos?

How can individuals protect themselves from falling victim to deepfake videos?

Detecting and flagging deepfake videos to prevent their spread requires a multi-pronged approach:

Technological Solutions

- **Advanced AI-powered tools:** Develop and utilize AI algorithms trained to analyze subtle inconsistencies in facial features, skin textures, lighting, movements, and lip-syncing within deepfakes.
- **Biometric and voice analysis:** Analyze eye movements, blinking patterns, voice patterns, and speech rhythms for discrepancies between the video/audio and the real person.
- **Reverse image search:** Integrate and improve reverse image search tools to trace the origin of manipulated images or videos used in deepfakes.
- **Digital forensics and watermarking:** Utilize forensics techniques to analyze video metadata and embed invisible watermarks in original content for easier verification.
- **Temporal analysis:** Examine video sequences for inconsistencies in movement and lighting across frames, a telltale sign of manipulation.

Social Media Platforms

- **Deploy sophisticated detection tools:** Implement AI-powered detection tools to flag suspicious content and proactively remove confirmed deepfakes.

- **Transparency and labeling:** Label AI-generated content and disclose potential use of deepfakes to increase user awareness and critical thinking.
- **Fact-checking partnerships:** Collaborate with established fact-checking organizations to verify claims and debunk deepfakes within their platforms.
- **User reporting and flagging:** Streamline reporting mechanisms for suspicious content and empower users to flag potential deepfakes.
- **Promoting diverse perspectives:** Prioritize reliable news outlets and diverse content in news feeds and search results to counter the spread of disinformation and echo chambers.

Individual Action

- **Critical thinking and skepticism:** Don't accept sensational or emotionally charged content at face value. Develop healthy skepticism towards online video, especially those with political or personal implications.
- **Source awareness and verification:** Check the credibility, track record, and potential biases of content creators and platforms. Look for corroborating evidence from reliable sources.
- **Analyze content for inconsistencies:** Examine visuals for unrealistic movements, lighting glitches, facial morphing, and inconsistencies in lip-syncing or voice patterns.
- **Consider timing and context:** Analyze whether the content aligns with current events or aims to manipulate opinions towards a specific agenda.
- **Engage in fact-checking:** Utilize fact-checking websites and tools to verify claims and identify potential manipulation. Don't hesitate to report suspicious content.

Legal Measures:

Several countries are considering or establishing legal frameworks to address the misuse of deepfakes:

- **Germany:** The country criminalized the creation and distribution of deepfakes used to harm someone's reputation or interfere with elections.
- **Singapore:** Strict laws prohibit the creation and distribution of deepfakes for various malicious purposes, including defamation, fraud, and public harm.
- **California:** The state recently enacted a law protecting individuals from having their likeness used in deepfakes without their consent, particularly in contexts like pornography or commercial endorsements.

However, developing global legal frameworks remains a complex issue due to differences in privacy laws, free speech principles, and definitions of harm.

Remember, individual vigilance and collective efforts are crucial in combating the spread of deepfakes. By actively questioning, verifying, and reporting suspicious content, we can empower ourselves and build a safer online environment where truth and authenticity prevail.

What are some potential real-world scenarios where deepfakes could be more persuasive?

Are there any other studies or research that support or contradict these findings?

How can we effectively educate people about the potential manipulation of deepfakes?

Deepfakes hold the potential to be highly persuasive in several real-world scenarios due to their ability to exploit human trust and cognitive biases. Here are some examples:

1. Misinformation and Politics

- **Fabricated statements or endorsements:** Deepfakes could be used to create videos of politicians saying things they never did, potentially impacting elections or swaying public opinion on critical issues.
- **Sabotaging campaigns:** Deepfakes of opponents engaging in offensive or inappropriate behavior could damage their reputation and influence voter perceptions.
- **Creating false narratives:** Manipulated videos of events or news reports could be used to spread misinformation and propaganda, further polarizing public discourse.

2. Financial Fraud and Scams

- **Impersonation for social engineering:** Deepfakes could be used to impersonate CEOs or company executives to defraud investors or trick employees into divulging sensitive information.

- **Fake video calls or voice recordings:** Deepfakes could be used to mimic voices and appearances for requesting unauthorized financial transactions or manipulating business deals.
- **Deepfake blackmail or extortion:** Videos manipulated to depict illegal or embarrassing acts could be used to blackmail individuals or coerce them into giving up money or resources.

3. Social Manipulation and Personal Harm

- **Revenge porn and defamation:** Deepfakes could be used to create sexually explicit or humiliating videos of individuals, causing immense personal distress and reputational damage.
- **Catfishing and online scams:** Deepfakes could be used to create false personas to manipulate online relationships, extract personal information, or even solicit money from unsuspecting victims.
- **Eroding trust in personal relationships:** Deepfakes can be used to fabricate evidence of infidelity or misconduct, potentially causing significant disruption and emotional harm within families and communities.

These are just a few examples, and the potential applications of deepfakes for persuasion and manipulation are likely to evolve as the technology advances. Research suggests that deepfakes can indeed be highly persuasive:

- **A study by Stanford University** found that viewers were more likely to believe a deepfake of a real person expressing an opinion compared to a text message or a person they didn't know.
- **Another study by MIT** showed that deepfakes can evoke stronger emotional responses than text or static images, increasing their potential impact on viewers.

However, it's important to note that other research indicates limitations to deepfake persuasiveness:

- **Studies by the University of Southern California** have shown that viewers with higher media literacy can better detect deepfakes and are less likely to be persuaded by them.
- **Research by the University of Warwick** suggests that awareness of deepfakes can act as a cognitive countermeasure, prompting viewers to be more skeptical and scrutinize content more critically.

Therefore, **education and media literacy** are crucial tools in combating the persuasive power of deepfakes. Here are some effective ways to educate people:

- **Interactive workshops and trainings:** Engaging workshops that involve analyzing real-world deepfakes and teaching techniques for identifying manipulation can raise awareness and develop critical thinking skills.
- **Educational resources and awareness campaigns:** Developing accessible online resources, infographics, and public awareness campaigns can inform a wider audience about the dangers of deepfakes and how to protect themselves.
- **Integrating media literacy into curriculums:** Educating students at all levels about online safety, critical thinking, and source evaluation can equip them with the necessary skills to navigate the digital world safely and responsibly.
- **Open discussions and community engagement:** Fostering open conversations and dialogues within communities about the potential harm of deepfakes and encouraging collective action against misinformation can build resilience and promote responsible online behavior.

By embracing these educational approaches and remaining vigilant, we can mitigate the persuasive power of deepfakes and create a more informed and empowered society in the face of this evolving technology.

What are some potential strategies that can be implemented to combat the spread of deepfakes?

How can media literacy education be effectively incorporated to help individuals identify deepfakes?

What are some other potential consequences of declining trust in media due to deepfakes?

Combating the spread of deepfakes and their negative consequences requires a multi-layered approach across technology, education, and social responsibility. Here are some potential strategies:

Technological Solutions

- **Advanced AI-powered detection tools:** Develop and utilize AI algorithms trained to identify subtle inconsistencies in facial features, movements, lighting, and lip-syncing within deepfakes.
- **Digital forensics and watermarking:** Utilize forensics techniques to analyze video metadata and embed invisible watermarks in original content for easier verification.
- **Reverse image search:** Integrate and improve reverse image search tools to trace the origin of manipulated images or videos used in deepfakes.
- **Open-source detection tools:** Develop and make freely available tools for deepfake detection, particularly in countries with limited resources.

Media Literacy Education

- **Interactive workshops and trainings:** Conduct workshops that involve analyzing real-world deepfakes and teaching techniques for identifying manipulation, focusing on critical thinking and source verification.

- **Educational resources and awareness campaigns:** Develop accessible online resources, infographics, and public awareness campaigns to inform people about the dangers of deepfakes and how to protect themselves.
- **Integration into curriculums:** Incorporate media literacy education into school curriculums at all levels, equipping students with the skills to analyze information, identify bias, and verify sources.
- **Community outreach and engagement:** Organize workshops and discussions within communities, particularly vulnerable groups, to raise awareness and promote responsible online behavior.

Social Responsibility

- **Content moderation and platform transparency:** Social media platforms need to implement robust content moderation systems with AI-powered detection tools and transparent reporting mechanisms for suspicious content.
- **Fact-checking partnerships:** Collaborate with fact-checking organizations to verify claims and debunk deepfakes directly on platforms.
- **Responsible AI development:** Promote ethical standards and guidelines for AI development and ensure responsible use of deepfake technology.
- **Legal frameworks and accountability:** Develop and enforce legal frameworks to address the harmful use of deepfakes, holding creators and distributors accountable for their actions.

Consequences of Declining Media Trust

- **Erosion of democracy and social cohesion:** Widespread distrust in media could lead to increased polarization, manipulation of public opinion, and difficulty discerning reliable information, impacting democracies and social harmony.

- **Exacerbation of misinformation and disinformation:** Deepfakes can fuel the spread of misinformation and disinformation campaigns, hindering accurate information dissemination and critical thinking.
- **Chilling effect on journalism and free speech:** Fear of manipulation through deepfakes might discourage journalists from reporting sensitive information or lead to self-censorship, impacting freedom of expression and access to reliable news.
- **Increased societal distrust and skepticism:** A pervasive environment of doubt and lack of trust in media can negatively impact societal interactions, public engagement, and collective decision-making.

By implementing these strategies and fostering collaboration among tech companies, educators, researchers, policymakers, and individuals, we can build a more resilient and informed society equipped to navigate the challenges of deepfakes and protect against their potential harm. Remember, collective efforts and individual vigilance are crucial in mitigating the negative impacts of deepfakes and safeguarding trust in information and communication.

What are some of the challenges in creating convincing deepfakes?

How do online platforms moderate and fact-check deepfakes?

What are some examples of manipulation and propaganda that have been around for centuries?

Challenges in Creating Convincing Deepfakes

Creating truly convincing deepfakes still presents several challenges:

1. Technical Limitations

- **Data requirements:** Large amounts of high-quality training data of the target person are needed, including various expressions, lighting conditions, and poses.
- **Unrealistic movements:** Subtle inconsistencies in facial expressions, lip-syncing, and body movements can still give away a deepfake.
- **Audio manipulation challenges:** Creating realistic-sounding synthetic voices that match the target's speech patterns and emotional nuances is difficult.
- **Detection and removal:** Advancements in deepfake detection tools pose a constant challenge for creators.

2. Ethical and Legal Considerations

- **Consent and authorization:** Obtaining informed consent from the target person for using their likeness can be complicated, especially for public figures.

- **Potential for misuse:** Deepfakes can be used for malicious purposes like defamation, blackmail, or spreading misinformation, raising ethical and legal concerns.
- **Attribution and transparency:** Identifying the creator and origin of deepfakes can be challenging, hindering accountability and transparency.

3. Availability of Resources

- **Software and hardware costs:** High-end computing resources and advanced software are needed to create high-quality deepfakes, limiting accessibility for individuals with limited resources.
- **Technical expertise:** Creating convincing deepfakes requires technical knowledge and skills in AI, video editing, and audio manipulation, further restricting widespread adoption.

Online Platform Moderation and Fact-Checking of Deepfakes

Moderation

- **AI-powered detection tools:** Platforms utilize algorithms trained to identify suspicious characteristics in videos, like unrealistic facial movements or inconsistencies in lighting and lip-syncing.
- **Human review teams:** Trained teams of reviewers analyze flagged content and decide on removal based on platform policies and potential harm.
- **User reporting mechanisms:** Platforms provide ways for users to report suspected deepfakes, allowing community participation in moderation efforts.

Fact-Checking

- **Partnerships with fact-checking organizations:** Platforms collaborate with independent fact-checkers to verify claims and debunk false information associated with deepfakes.
- **Contextual analysis and verification:** Fact-checkers analyze the content, source, and potential motivations behind deepfakes to assess their authenticity and impact.
- **Labeling and warnings:** Platforms might label suspected deepfakes or provide warnings to users to raise awareness and encourage critical thinking.

Examples of Historical Manipulation and Propaganda

While deepfakes represent a new form of manipulation, the concept of using false information and propaganda to influence individuals and societies has existed for centuries:

- **Political Cartoons and Caricatures:** Throughout history, political cartoons and caricatures have been used to exaggerate features and ridicule opponents, often with the aim of swaying public opinion.
- **Fake News and Fabricated Accounts:** Inventing news stories and manipulating historical accounts have been used for centuries to influence political outcomes, create fear, or legitimize specific claims.
- **Staged Photographs and Altered Images:** Manipulating photographs through airbrushing, compositing, and other techniques has been used to distort reality and control narratives, even before the digital age.
- **Misinformation and Propaganda Campaigns:** Orchestrated campaigns to spread misinformation and propaganda have been employed by governments and organizations for centuries, aiming to control public perception and shape narratives.

The rise of deepfakes presents a new level of sophistication and potential for harm in creating manipulated content. However, understanding the historical context of misinformation and propaganda can help us identify patterns, develop critical thinking skills, and build resilience against these evolving forms of manipulation.

Remember, critical thinking, awareness of historical manipulation techniques, and a healthy dose of skepticism are crucial tools in navigating the information landscape, whether facing deepfakes or other forms of misinformation.

What are some potential ways to detect and combat the spread of shallow fakes?

How can social media platforms like Facebook better address the issue of shallow fakes?

Are there any legal or regulatory measures in place to address the spread of shallow fakes?

Detecting and Combating Shallow Fakes

Combating shallow fakes requires a multi-pronged approach:

Technological Solutions

- **Reverse image search and verification tools:** Implement robust reverse image search tools integrated into platforms to allow users to quickly verify the origin of images and identify manipulated content.
- **Fact-checking partnerships:** Collaborate with fact-checking organizations to develop automated content analysis tools that flag content containing known misinformation or inconsistent claims.
- **AI-powered anomaly detection:** Train AI algorithms to identify suspicious patterns in image manipulation, like unnatural lighting, inconsistencies in shadows, or text alterations.
- **Open-source verification tools:** Develop and make accessible open-source tools for verifying content, particularly in regions with limited resources.

Social Media Platform Strategies

- **Contextual analysis and labeling:** Analyze content for misleading captions, framing, and omissions, providing labels or warnings to alert users of potential bias or manipulation.
- **Promotion of reliable sources:** Prioritize and amplify content from established and reputable sources in news feeds and search results, reducing visibility of manipulative content.
- **User education and awareness campaigns:** Launch campaigns educating users about identifying shallow fakes, focusing on critical thinking, source verification, and healthy skepticism.
- **Improved content moderation:** Invest in human review teams trained to identify and remove harmful content, including shallow fakes used for defamation, disinformation, or hate speech.

Individual Action

- **Critical thinking and skepticism:** Develop a healthy level of skepticism towards online content, particularly emotionally charged or highly sensational material.
- **Source verification and cross-checking:** Check the source, author, and publication date of content, cross-referencing information with reliable sources.
- **Reverse image search and fact-checking tools:** Utilize reverse image search tools and fact-checking resources to verify the authenticity of claims and images.
- **Reporting suspicious content:** Actively report content suspected of being manipulated or containing misinformation to platform moderators.

Facebook's Approach to Shallow Fakes

Facebook has implemented several measures to address shallow fakes:

- **Third-party fact-checking partnerships:** Facebook collaborates with independent fact-checkers to verify claims and label disputed content.

- **Independent Oversight Board:** The board reviews appeals from users regarding content removal decisions, including cases involving manipulated content.
- **AI-powered detection tools:** Facebook utilizes AI systems to identify potentially harmful content, including manipulated images and videos.
- **Transparency initiatives:** Facebook has launched initiatives to promote transparency around content moderation decisions and algorithms.

However, challenges remain:

- **Accuracy of AI detection:** AI systems can struggle to differentiate between legitimate edits and manipulative alterations.
- **Scale and volume of content:** Facebook faces immense challenges in moderating the enormous amount of content uploaded daily.
- **Misinformation campaigns:** Malicious actors constantly adapt their tactics, making it difficult for platforms to stay ahead of the curve.

Legal and Regulatory Measures

Several countries are considering or implementing legal measures to address the spread of online misinformation, including:

- **Germany:** The NetzDG law holds social media platforms accountable for removing illegal content, including manipulated content used to cause harm.
- **Singapore:** The Online Falsehoods Manipulation Act criminalizes the creation and spread of false or misleading information online.
- **France:** The Avia law requires platforms to remove hateful content within 24 hours of notification.

While these measures aim to address misinformation in general, specific legal frameworks surrounding shallow fakes are still evolving. The challenge lies in balancing freedom of expression with the need to protect individuals and societies from harmful manipulation.

A combined effort from tech companies, governments, educators, and individuals is crucial in effectively combating the spread of shallow fakes. By promoting critical thinking, utilizing verification tools, and demanding accountable platform policies, we can work towards a safer and more informed online environment.

What are some potential risks or consequences of deepfake technology becoming more accessible in the future?

How do you think the democratization of deepfake technology will impact society and individuals?

Are there any measures being taken to regulate or control the use of deepfake technology?

The increasing accessibility of deepfake technology poses several potential risks and consequences, both for individuals and society as a whole. Here are some key concerns:

Individual Risks

- **Erosion of trust and credibility:** Deepfakes can be used to fabricate compromising videos or statements, damaging personal reputations and relationships. This can lead to anxiety, fear, and difficulty discerning truth from falsehood.
- **Blackmail and extortion:** Malicious actors could use deepfakes to blackmail individuals with fabricated evidence, leading to financial losses or emotional distress.
- **Identity theft and fraud:** Deepfakes could be used to impersonate individuals for financial gain or to gain access to restricted information or systems.
- **Psychological manipulation and harassment:** Deepfakes can be used to create emotionally charged content for trolling, cyberbullying, or spreading misinformation. This can have significant negative impacts on mental health and emotional well-being.

Societal Risks

- **Rise of disinformation and propaganda:** Deepfakes could be used to manipulate public opinion on critical issues, influence elections, and fuel social unrest. This can further polarize societies and erode trust in institutions.
- **Damage to democracy and free speech:** The ability to easily fabricate evidence and manipulate narratives could threaten democratic processes and limit free speech by creating a chilling effect on public discourse.
- **Erosion of social cohesion and trust:** Deepfakes can exacerbate existing divisions and conflicts within societies by amplifying distrust and suspicion between different groups.
- **Economic losses and harm to businesses:** Deepfakes can be used to damage corporate reputations, manipulate financial markets, and disrupt business operations.

Democratization and Societal Impact

While the increasing accessibility of deepfake technology could provide opportunities for creative expression and artistic exploration, it also raises concerns about its potential misuse by individuals with malicious intent. Some potential impacts include:

- **Empowerment for marginalized voices:** Deepfakes could offer new tools for marginalized groups to express themselves and raise awareness about important issues.
- **Blurring of the lines between reality and fiction:** Widespread access to deepfakes could erode our ability to discern truth from falsehood, making it increasingly difficult to navigate the information landscape.
- **Rise of "fake news" and hyper-partisanship:** Deepfakes could be used to further entrench people in their existing beliefs and create echo chambers, making it harder to engage in respectful discourse and find common ground.

Regulation and Control Measures

Several measures are being considered to regulate and control the use of deepfake technology:

- **Legal frameworks:** Some countries are developing laws to criminalize the creation and distribution of deepfakes for malicious purposes, such as defamation, fraud, or incitement to violence.
- **Platform responsibilities:** Social media platforms and content creators are facing increasing pressure to develop and implement more robust content moderation policies and detection tools to identify and remove harmful deepfakes.
- **Technological solutions:** Researchers are developing AI-powered tools to detect and debunk deepfakes, but these technologies are still evolving and raise concerns about potential biases and limitations.
- **Media literacy and education:** Educating individuals about deepfakes, how to identify them, and how to critically evaluate information online is crucial in mitigating their harmful effects.

The development of ethical guidelines and standards for the use of deepfake technology is also essential. However, finding the right balance between regulating harmful uses and protecting freedom of expression remains a complex challenge.

Addressing the risks associated with deepfakes requires a comprehensive approach that involves individual vigilance, technological advancements, legal frameworks, and collective efforts to promote media literacy and ethical use of this powerful technology.

How can intelligence agencies effectively detect and mitigate the risks associated with deepfake videos?

Are there any specific strategies or technologies that can be used to counter deepfake disinformation operations?

What are some potential consequences or risks associated with the use of deepfake videos in disinformation campaigns?

Detecting and mitigating the risks of deepfake videos in disinformation campaigns presents a significant challenge for intelligence agencies. Here are some potential strategies and technologies they can employ:

Detection

- **Advanced AI-powered tools:** Develop and utilize AI algorithms trained to analyze subtle inconsistencies in deepfakes, like facial movements, lip-syncing, lighting, and pixelation patterns.
- **Forensic analysis:** Employ specialists to analyze metadata, video compression artifacts, and inconsistencies in audio frequencies to identify signs of manipulation.
- **Open-source intelligence:** Monitor social media and online platforms for suspicious trends, keywords, and coordinated campaigns that might involve deepfakes.
- **Human intelligence:** Utilize human analysts with expertise in specific regions, actors, and disinformation tactics to detect deepfakes within their areas of focus.

Mitigation

- **Counter-narrative campaigns:** Develop and disseminate factual information and evidence debunking deepfakes to limit their reach and impact.

- **Public awareness and education:** Train journalists, public officials, and the general public to recognize deepfakes and critically evaluate information online.
- **Collaboration with platforms:** Work with social media companies and content creators to improve detection and removal of harmful deepfakes on their platforms.
- **International cooperation:** Foster international collaboration among intelligence agencies and governments to share information, best practices, and counter-deepfake technologies.

Specific Technologies

- **Reverse image and video search tools:** Utilize advanced search engines to identify the origin of images and video footage used in deepfakes, tracing them back to potential sources.
- **Biometric and voice analysis tools:** Analyze facial features, eye movements, and voice patterns for discrepancies between the real person and the deepfake video.
- **Temporal analysis tools:** Examine video sequences for inconsistencies in movement, lighting, and shadows throughout the footage, often telltale signs of manipulation.
- **Digital watermarking and authentication technologies:** Embed invisible watermarks or tamper-proof signatures in original content to verify its authenticity.

Risks of Deepfake Disinformation Campaigns

- **Erosion of trust and credibility:** Deepfakes can erode trust in institutions, media, and even individuals, weakening social cohesion and hindering public discourse.
- **Manipulation of public opinion:** Malicious actors can use deepfakes to sway public opinion on critical issues, influence elections, and fuel social unrest.

- **Damage to reputations and relationships:** Fabricated deepfakes can be used to damage the reputations of individuals, organizations, and even entire countries.
- **Exacerbation of existing conflicts and divisions:** Deepfakes can be used to amplify existing tensions and conflicts within societies, potentially leading to violence and instability.
- **Chilling effect on free speech and dissent:** Fear of deepfake manipulation might discourage individuals from expressing their opinions or participating in public discourse.

Combating deepfakes requires a multi-pronged approach combining technological advancements, intelligence gathering, public awareness campaigns, and international cooperation. By investing in these efforts, intelligence agencies and other stakeholders can help limit the negative impacts of deepfake disinformation and safeguard against these evolving threats.

Remember, effective countermeasures also require individual vigilance and responsible online behavior. We must all remain critical consumers of information, verify sources, and report suspicious content to help create a safer and more informed online environment.

How can the limitations in acquiring training data for deepfakes be addressed?

Are there any alternative methods to create high-quality deepfakes without extensive training data?

What are some potential risks associated with the creation of deepfakes?

Addressing data limitations for deepfakes

Challenges

- **Privacy concerns:** Collecting real-world data raises ethical and legal issues about consent and privacy.
- **Biases:** Existing datasets can be biased in demographics, speech patterns, etc., leading to biased deepfakes.
- **Restricted access:** High-quality data can be proprietary or expensive, limiting access and fostering monopolies.

Solutions:

- **Synthetic data:** Generate realistic faces and voices from scratch, reducing privacy concerns and biases. However, achieving realism and diversity remains challenging.
- **Transfer learning:** Leverage pre-trained models on general datasets for specific tasks, improving efficiency but still requiring some additional data collection.
- **Few-shot learning:** Techniques to learn from very few examples help personalize deepfakes with limited data, but require more complex model architectures.
- **Data augmentation:** Artificially modify existing data (e.g., changing lighting, expressions) to increase diversity and generalize better.

High-quality deepfakes with less data

- **Better model architectures:** Develop models that learn more efficiently from limited data using techniques like attention mechanisms and meta-learning.
- **Domain-specific data:** Focus on collecting smaller datasets specific to the desired application (e.g., medical images, historical figures) for better performance.
- **Active learning:** Models can query for specific data points they need most for improvement, optimizing data collection.

Potential risks of deepfakes

- **Misinformation and disinformation:** Spreading false information, manipulating public opinion, undermining trust in institutions.
- **Reputation damage:** Falsely implicating individuals in harmful situations, leading to personal and professional consequences.
- **Fraud and scams:** Impersonating individuals for financial gain or manipulating financial markets.
- **Social and political manipulation:** Influencing elections, sowing discord, exacerbating societal divisions.
- **Psychological harm:** Creating anxiety, fear, or distrust among individuals and communities.

Mitigating the risks

- **Detection and verification technologies:** Develop robust tools to identify and verify deepfakes to counteract their harmful impact.
- **Media literacy and education:** Empower individuals to critically evaluate online content and recognize deepfakes.
- **Ethical guidelines and regulations:** Establish clear ethical standards and legal frameworks for deepfake development and use.

- **Transparency and accountability:** Encourage creators to disclose deepfake content as such and hold them accountable for misuse.

Remember, deepfakes have both potential benefits and significant risks. Addressing data limitations through alternative methods and focusing on responsible development and use are crucial for shaping a positive future for this technology.

How can developers and security researchers stay ahead of adversaries who exploit zero-day vulnerabilities in deepfake technology?

What are some potential strategies for improving the accuracy and efficiency of deepfake detection tools?

How can media literacy programs help individuals recognize and resist the influence of deepfakes?

Staying ahead of deepfake vulnerabilities

Developers and security researchers can employ several strategies to stay ahead of zero-day vulnerabilities:

- **Formal verification:** Using mathematical methods to prove software's correctness eliminates entire classes of vulnerabilities.
- **Fuzzing and mutation testing:** Throwing unexpected inputs at the software and analyzing its behavior helps identify hidden flaws.
- **Threat modeling and adversarial training:** Simulating attacker behavior and training the software to defend against it strengthens its resilience.
- **Open-source development:** Fostering a global community to review and improve code increases the chances of spotting vulnerabilities.
- **Continuous monitoring and patching:** Regularly scanning systems for newly discovered vulnerabilities and deploying patches promptly is crucial.

Improving deepfake detection tools

Accuracy and efficiency of detection tools can be enhanced through:

- **Multimodal analysis:** Considering audio, video, text, and other modalities together strengthens detection compared to analyzing each aspect separately.
- **Temporal coherence analysis:** Checking for inconsistencies in movement, speech patterns, and lighting across frames unveils deepfakes.
- **AI-powered anomaly detection:** Employing machine learning models trained on real and fake data to identify suspicious patterns.
- **Reverse engineering of deepfake models:** Understanding how attackers create deepfakes helps build better detectors.
- **Collaboration and data sharing:** Sharing detection models and deepfake samples within the research community accelerates progress.

Media literacy for deepfake resistance

Media literacy programs can empower individuals to recognize and resist deepfakes by:

- **Teaching critical thinking skills:** Analyzing sources, verifying information, and questioning claims equip individuals to evaluate content objectively.
- **Highlighting common deepfake techniques:** Raising awareness of manipulation techniques like lip-syncing, facial warping, and voice cloning helps identify signs of fakery.
- **Providing practical tools and resources:** Offering online fact-checking platforms, reverse image search tools, and browser extensions for suspicious content alerts empowers individuals to verify information.
- **Promoting healthy skepticism:** Encouraging questioning of online content and avoiding impulsive reactions to sensationalized narratives reduces susceptibility to manipulation.
- **Encouraging source awareness:** Recognizing trusted sources and verifying author credentials cultivates a more cautious approach to online information.

By adopting these strategies, developers, researchers, and individuals can collectively mitigate the risks associated with deepfakes and harness the technology for positive purposes. Remember, a collaborative approach that prioritizes security, transparency, and education is crucial to navigating the complex landscape of deepfakes in the digital age.

What are some of the techniques being developed to detect deepfakes?

Are there any regulations or standards in place to address the misuse of deepfakes?

How can individuals protect themselves from the potential harm caused by deepfakes?

Deepfake Detection Techniques

- **Multimodal Analysis:** Analyzing audio, video, text, and other modalities together to identify inconsistencies in lip-syncing, speech patterns, and background elements.
- **Temporal Coherence Analysis:** Examining consecutive frames for unnatural transitions, lighting changes, or flickering pixels to detect manipulated sequences.
- **AI-powered Anomaly Detection:** Machine learning models trained on real and fake data can identify subtle anomalies in facial expressions, blinking patterns, and body movements.
- **Forensic Traces:** Exploiting compression artifacts, metadata inconsistencies, and telltale traces of editing software to reveal manipulation.
- **Reverse Engineering Deepfake Models:** Understanding how deepfakes are created helps develop targeted detection algorithms to identify specific manipulation techniques.

Regulations and Standards

Currently, there are no comprehensive regulations or standards specific to deepfakes. However, some initiatives attempt to address their misuse:

- **EU's Digital Services Act:** Requires large online platforms to implement measures against "manipulated content" and misinformation.
- **California's Deepfakes Law:** Requires disclosure of manipulated audio and video in political campaigns.
- **Industry Initiatives:** Tech companies like Adobe and Microsoft are developing tools and policies to promote transparency and responsible use of AI.

Protecting Yourself from Deepfakes

- **Media Literacy:** Develop critical thinking skills, question online content, verify information through trusted sources, and be aware of common deepfake techniques.
- **Source Awareness:** Be cautious of unfamiliar sources, check author credentials, and verify claims through reputable news outlets.
- **Reverse Image Search:** Use tools like Tineye or Google Images to check if visuals have been used elsewhere online.
- **Browser Extensions:** Utilize browser extensions that flag potentially manipulated content or offer fact-checking features.
- **Healthy Skepticism:** Maintain a healthy skepticism towards sensationalized claims and avoid sharing unverified information.

Remember, the responsibility to combat deepfakes lies not only with developers and policymakers but also with individuals practicing media literacy and responsible online behavior. By staying informed, vigilant, and skeptical, we can navigate the digital landscape with greater awareness and protect ourselves from potential harm.

What are some specific detection techniques that are being developed to identify deepfakes?

How can media literacy be effectively promoted to help individuals identify and resist the influence of deepfakes?

Can you provide examples of regulatory initiatives that have been implemented to address the issue of deepfakes?

Specific Deepfake Detection Techniques

Video/Image-Based

- **Facial Landmark Analysis:** Analyze the movement and consistency of facial landmarks (eyes, nose, mouth) to detect unnatural warping or jitter.
- **Blink Detection:** Analyze blinking patterns for inconsistencies in frequency, duration, and symmetry, as deepfakes often struggle with realistic blinks.
- **Skin Tone and Texture Analysis:** Identify inconsistencies in skin tone and texture across frames, as deepfakes can struggle with lighting and shadows.
- **Artifacts and Anomalies:** Detect subtle artifacts like compression errors, flickering pixels, or unnatural blurring, which can indicate manipulation.
- **Temporal Consistency Analysis:** Examine the movement of objects and shadows across frames to identify inconsistencies or jerky motions suggestive of manipulation.

Audio-Based

- **Mel-Frequency Cepstral Coefficients (MFCCs):** Analyze the spectral characteristics of speech to detect inconsistencies in voice patterns or lip-syncing mismatch.

- **Forensic Audio Analysis:** Identify audio artifacts or inconsistencies in background noise, microphone characteristics, or room acoustics.
- **Speaker Recognition:** Compare voice features to known recordings to identify potential impersonation or synthetic voices.

Hybrid Techniques

- **Multimodal Analysis:** Combine video, audio, and text analysis to detect inconsistencies across modalities and strengthen detection accuracy.
- **AI-powered Anomaly Detection:** Train machine learning models on large datasets of real and fake data to identify subtle anomalies in various modalities.
- **Deepfake Model Fingerprinting:** Analyze the underlying structure of deepfake models to identify specific manipulation techniques or creators.

Promoting Media Literacy for Deepfake Resistance

- **Educational Curriculums:** Integrate deepfake awareness into school curriculums, teaching students critical thinking, source evaluation, and fact-checking skills.
- **Public Awareness Campaigns:** Launch public awareness campaigns through media channels and social media platforms to educate the public about deepfakes, their techniques, and potential harms.
- **Interactive Workshops and Games:** Develop interactive workshops and games that challenge individuals to identify deepfakes in real-world scenarios, improving their detection skills in a fun and engaging way.
- **Fact-Checking Platforms and Tools:** Support and promote the development of accessible fact-checking platforms and tools that individuals can easily use to verify information and identify manipulated content.

- **Collaboration with Social Media Platforms:** Encourage social media platforms to incorporate educational resources and features into their platforms to raise awareness and empower users to identify and report deepfakes.

Regulatory Initiatives

- **EU's Digital Services Act (DSA):** Requires large online platforms to implement measures against "manipulated content" and misinformation, including deepfakes. This includes takedown mechanisms, user reporting systems, and transparency around algorithms used to detect and flag such content.
- **California's Deepfakes Law:** Requires the disclosure of manipulated audio and video content used in political campaigns, aiming to increase transparency and prevent the spread of disinformation during elections.
- **Singapore's Online Falsehoods Act:** Empowers authorities to remove or correct online content deemed false or misleading, including deepfakes. This raises concerns about censorship and potential misuse by the government.
- **Industry Initiatives:** Tech companies like Adobe and Microsoft are developing tools and policies to promote transparency and responsible use of AI, including features to identify and flag potential deepfakes within their software.

Remember, tackling deepfakes requires a multi-pronged approach. Combining advanced detection techniques, proactive media literacy initiatives, and effective regulations can help us navigate this complex challenge and mitigate the potential harms of deepfakes on individuals and society.

How do these automated systems detect deepfake videos?

What are some challenges in developing effective discriminators to detect deepfake content?

Are there any other approaches besides developing automated systems to mitigate the rise of deepfakes?

Automated systems use various techniques to detect deepfakes, often analyzing different aspects of the video and audio:

Video-based techniques

- **Facial landmark analysis:** Tracking and analyzing movements of key facial features like eyes, nose, and mouth to identify unnatural warping or jitter.
- **Blink detection:** Analyzing frequency, duration, and symmetry of blinks, as deepfakes often struggle with realistic blinking patterns.
- **Skin tone and texture analysis:** Detecting inconsistencies in skin tone and texture across frames, indicating potential manipulation due to lighting or shadow issues.
- **Artifacts and anomalies:** Looking for subtle artifacts like compression errors, flickering pixels, or unnatural blurring which can reveal manipulation.
- **Temporal consistency analysis:** Examining the movement of objects and shadows across frames to identify inconsistencies or jerky motions suggestive of manipulation.

Audio-based techniques

- **Mel-Frequency Cepstral Coefficients (MFCCs):** Analyzing the spectral characteristics of speech to detect inconsistencies in voice patterns or lip-syncing mismatch.
- **Forensic audio analysis:** Identifying audio artifacts or inconsistencies in background noise, microphone characteristics, or room acoustics.
- **Speaker recognition:** Comparing voice features to known recordings to identify potential impersonation or synthetic voices.

Combined techniques

- **Multimodal analysis:** Combining video, audio, and text analysis to identify inconsistencies across modalities and strengthen detection accuracy.
- **AI-powered anomaly detection:** Machine learning models trained on large datasets of real and fake data to identify subtle anomalies across various modalities.
- **Deepfake model fingerprinting:** Analyzing the underlying structure of deepfake models to identify specific manipulation techniques or creators.

Challenges in developing effective discriminators

- **Evolving deepfake technology:** Deepfakes are constantly improving, making it difficult for static detectors to keep up.
- **Limited training data:** Effective detectors require large amounts of high-quality data, which can be expensive and difficult to obtain.
- **Bias and fairness:** Detectors trained on biased datasets may perform poorly on certain demographics or content types.
- **Privacy concerns:** Collecting and using training data raises privacy concerns and ethical considerations.

Alternative approaches to mitigating deepfakes:

- **Media literacy education:** Empowering individuals to critically evaluate online content, recognize common deepfake techniques, and verify information through trusted sources.
- **Transparency and disclosure:** Encouraging creators and platforms to disclose manipulated content, allowing users to make informed decisions about the information they consume.
- **Regulation and policy:** Developing legal frameworks and industry standards to address the misuse of deepfakes and hold individuals or platforms accountable.
- **Supporting alternative technologies:** Promoting the development of secure and tamper-proof technologies like blockchain or cryptographic verification methods to authenticate digital content.

Remember, effective deepfake detection and mitigation require a multifaceted approach. Combining advanced technologies, education, awareness, and ethical practices can help us build a more responsible and trustworthy digital landscape.

How can researchers and developers stay ahead of the deepfake threat given the rapid advancements in deepfake technology?

Are there any promising approaches or strategies being explored to improve deepfake detection capabilities?

What are the potential consequences of deepfakes becoming indistinguishable from real images?

Staying Ahead of the Deepfake Threat

Researchers and developers face a constant race against the advancements in deepfake technology. Here are some strategies to stay ahead:

- **Continual Monitoring and Adaptation:** Closely monitor the evolution of deepfake techniques and constantly update detection algorithms to identify new manipulation methods.
- **Adversarial Training:** Train detection models on synthetic deepfakes created by simulating potential attacker strategies, making them more resilient to future attacks.
- **Open-source Collaboration:** Foster an open-source community for detection research and development, allowing rapid sharing of ideas and advancements.
- **Focus on Explainable AI:** Develop explainable deepfake detection models that not only identify manipulated content but also explain how they reached their conclusions, aiding in understanding and countering new techniques.
- **Interdisciplinary Approach:** Combine expertise from fields like computer vision, audio processing, machine learning, and psychology to develop comprehensive detection solutions.

Promising Approaches for Improved Detection

- **Multimodal Fusion:** Integrate the analysis of video, audio, and text modalities to achieve more robust detection by identifying inconsistencies across different data sources.
- **Temporal Coherence Analysis:** Analyze the relationships between elements across consecutive frames to detect unnatural transitions, lighting changes, or inconsistencies in movement, revealing manipulation.
- **Deepfake Model Fingerprinting:** Identify the fingerprints of specific deepfake models used to create content, allowing for targeted detection and attribution of manipulated media.
- **Biometric and Physiological Signal Analysis:** Analyze subtle biometric and physiological signals like heartbeat or pupil dilation, as deepfakes often struggle to replicate these nuances.
- **Leveraging Physics and Realism Constraints:** Develop detection methods based on real-world physics and human limitations, identifying inconsistencies in shadows, reflections, or object interactions within manipulated videos.

Consequences of Indistinguishable Deepfakes

- **Widespread Misinformation and Disinformation:** Deepfakes could become so convincing that they are indistinguishable from reality, leading to the spread of false information, swaying public opinion, and undermining trust in institutions.
- **Erosion of Social Cohesion:** Deepfakes could be used to create fake news, slander individuals, and sow discord within communities, potentially fueling social unrest and political polarization.

- **Financial Fraud and Scams:** Deepfakes could be used to impersonate individuals in financial transactions, manipulate financial markets, and commit other forms of fraud with devastating consequences.
- **Psychological Harm and Manipulation:** Deepfakes could be used to intimidate, blackmail, or embarrass individuals, causing emotional distress and potentially influencing their behavior.
- **Damage to Personal Reputation and Privacy:** Deepfakes could be used to create compromising situations or false narratives about individuals, irreparably damaging their reputations and violating their privacy.

It's crucial to develop robust detection technologies alongside media literacy programs, ethical guidelines, and legal frameworks to mitigate the potential harms of indistinguishable deepfakes and ensure responsible development and utilization of this technology for positive purposes.

What are some potential implications of the lower accuracy in detecting deepfakes from the black box dataset?

How can researchers address the challenges of detecting deepfakes in real-world scenarios?

Are there any specific techniques or approaches that have shown promise in improving the accuracy of deepfake detection?

Implications of Lower Accuracy with Black Box Deepfakes

- **Increased Difficulty in Mitigating Harms:** If detection tools struggle with black box deepfakes, identifying and removing harmful content becomes significantly harder, leading to wider circulation of misinformation and manipulated media.
- **Erosion of Trust in Detection Technology:** Public confidence in deepfake detection tools could erode if they consistently fail to identify black box creations, potentially causing people to become more susceptible to manipulated content.
- **Empowerment of Malicious Actors:** The difficulty of detecting black box deepfakes could embolden malicious actors to create and spread increasingly sophisticated manipulated media, further exacerbating societal and political issues.
- **Challenges for Law Enforcement and Policymakers:** The lack of reliable detection for black box deepfakes hinders efforts to enforce regulations against harmful content and hold individuals accountable for its creation and dissemination.

Addressing Challenges of Real-World Deepfake Detection

- **Adapting to Diverse Data:** Detection models need to be adaptive and trained on real-world data beyond controlled datasets to account for variations in lighting, camera angles, and other factors that affect video and audio quality.
- **Incorporating Context and Prior Knowledge:** Integrating contextual information like speaker identity, video location, and event details can enhance detection accuracy by identifying inconsistencies and red flags within the manipulated content.
- **Combating Adversarial Attacks:** Researchers need to develop detection methods that are resilient against adversarial attacks, where creators deliberately try to fool the algorithms by manipulating specific aspects of the deepfake.
- **Leveraging Explainable AI:** Implementing explainable AI techniques in detection models allows researchers to understand why the model identifies certain content as a deepfake, aiding in refining algorithms and addressing potential biases.
- **Collaborative Research and Data Sharing:** Fostering collaboration and data sharing between researchers, private companies, and government agencies can accelerate progress in developing robust detection tools and addressing the evolving landscape of deepfakes.

Promising Techniques for Improved Detection Accuracy

- **Multimodal Fusion:** Combining analysis of video, audio, text, and other modalities provides a more comprehensive view of the content and can reveal inconsistencies across different data sources, improving detection accuracy.

- **Temporal Coherence Analysis:** Examining the relationships between elements across consecutive frames can identify unnatural transitions, lighting changes, or inconsistencies in movement, revealing manipulation.
- **Deepfake Model Fingerprinting:** Identifying the fingerprints of specific deepfake models used to create content allows for targeted detection and attribution of manipulated media, enabling countermeasures against specific creators or techniques.
- **Biometric and Physiological Signal Analysis:** Analyzing subtle biometric and physiological signals like heartbeat or pupil dilation can uncover discrepancies between real and manipulated content, as deepfakes often struggle to replicate these nuances.
- **Leveraging Physics and Realism Constraints:** Developing detection methods based on real-world physics and human limitations can identify inconsistencies in shadows, reflections, or object interactions within manipulated videos.

Remember, overcoming the challenges of black box deepfakes and improving detection accuracy requires a multifaceted approach. Combining advanced research techniques, real-world data integration, explainable AI, and collaborative efforts can help us build robust detection systems and mitigate the potential harms of these evolving technologies.

What are some other initiatives that have been recommended to address the arms race between deepfake creation and detection?

How effective are detection algorithms in identifying deepfake content?

Are there any challenges or limitations in using social media platforms' image repositories for training detection programs?

Initiatives beyond detection

Beyond detection, various initiatives can address the deepfake arms race:

- **Media literacy education:** Equipping individuals to critically evaluate online content, recognize manipulation techniques, and verify information through trusted sources can decrease susceptibility to deepfakes.
- **Transparency and disclosure:** Encouraging creators and platforms to disclose manipulated content allows users to make informed decisions about the information they consume.
- **Regulation and policy:** Developing legal frameworks and industry standards to address the misuse of deepfakes and hold individuals or platforms accountable can deter malicious actors.
- **Supporting alternative technologies:** Promoting secure and tamper-proof technologies like blockchain or cryptographic verification methods can authenticate digital content and combat deepfakes at their source.
- **Focus on source code and training data:** Analyzing the source code of deepfake tools and the datasets used to train them can reveal vulnerabilities and biases, allowing for countermeasures and promoting responsible development.
- **Encouraging ethical development:** Emphasizing ethical considerations and responsible practices in deepfake creation and

research can prevent misuse and promote positive applications of the technology.

Detection algorithm effectiveness

Detection algorithms vary in accuracy depending on factors like dataset size, complexity of deepfakes, and implementation specifics. While no algorithm is perfect, advancements are promising:

- **Accuracy rates:** Some reports indicate state-of-the-art detectors approaching 90% accuracy on specific datasets, though performance can vary in real-world scenarios.
- **Generalization:** Challenges arise when dealing with diverse deepfakes created with different tools and techniques.
- **Continuous improvement:** Research and development efforts are ongoing, continuously improving detection capabilities and adapting to evolving deepfake technology.

Social media data for training

Using social media image repositories for training detection programs presents both potential and challenges:

- **Pros:** Large datasets offer diverse real-world content, potentially helping build robust detectors.
- **Cons:** Privacy concerns surrounding user data need careful consideration. Additionally, social media content may not be labeled as real or fake, requiring careful curation and verification.
- **Bias:** Datasets can reflect existing biases and may not generalize well to different demographics or content types.

Leveraging social media data requires careful ethical considerations, data anonymization practices, and diligent curation to maximize benefits while minimizing potential harm. Combining social media data with other sources can contribute to building more robust and adaptable detection models.

Remember, combatting deepfakes demands a multi-pronged approach. Beyond detection technologies, initiatives promoting media literacy, ethical development, and responsible use are crucial for ensuring a safe and trustworthy digital landscape.

Conclusion

Unveiling the Deepfake Dilemma: A Conclusion on Deception and Detection

We've traced the rapid evolution of this technology, from playful morphing apps to hyper-realistic manipulations capable of blurring the lines between truth and fiction. While this potential for creativity and expression holds undeniable allure, lurking within its shadows lies a darker side: the potential for widespread deception and social manipulation.

The challenge we face is clear: a seemingly endless arms race between the innovators creating ever-more convincing deepfakes and the researchers scrambling to develop robust detection tools. Yet, amidst this digital duel, glimmers of hope emerge. Advancements in fields like multimodal fusion, temporal coherence analysis, and explainable AI offer promising avenues for enhanced detection accuracy.

Yet, technology alone cannot bridge the widening gap between authenticity and manipulation. We must remember that the fight against deepfakes necessitates a more holistic approach, one that extends beyond the sterile walls of research labs and into the very fabric of our society. This is where initiatives like media literacy education, transparency and disclosure practices, and ethical development frameworks become the potent allies in our collective defense.

Equipping individuals with the critical thinking skills and digital savvy to discern truth from fabrication holds immense power. Empowering platforms to prioritize transparency and hold content creators accountable for malicious manipulation is another crucial step. Finally, fostering a culture of ethical development, where the potential benefits of deepfakes are harnessed responsibly and sustainably, is the cornerstone of navigating this technological frontier.

This journey has only just begun, and the complexities we've explored today will undoubtedly evolve. New deepfake techniques will emerge, demanding continuous innovation and adaptation in our detection methods. But by embracing collaboration, prioritizing ethical considerations, and cultivating a society armed with critical thinking, we can ensure that technology remains a tool for progress, not a weapon of deception.

Remember, the choice lies not with algorithms or algorithms, but with ourselves. It's our collective responsibility to ensure that the future of deepfakes is one where creativity flourishes but truth prevails. Let us continue the conversation, embrace a spirit of collaboration, and together, shape a digital landscape where technology empowers rather than deceives.

This is not just a conclusion, but an invitation to continue the dialogue, to challenge ourselves, and to collectively weave a tapestry of digital literacy and ethical responsibility. By doing so, we can ensure that the potential of deepfakes is harnessed for good, shaping a future where truth remains the north star guiding our way.

References

References

Agarwal, Sakshi, and Lav R. Varshney, "Limits of Deepfake Detection: A Robust Estimation Viewpoint," unpublished manuscript, arXiv:1905.03493, Version 1, May 9, 2019.

Ajder, Henry, Giorgio Patrini, Francesco Cavalli, and Laurence Cullen, *The State of Deepfakes: Landscape, Threats and Impact*, Amsterdam: Deeptrace, September 2019.

Atlantic Council's Digital Forensic Research Lab, "#Stop the Steal: Timeline of Social Media and Extremist Activities Leading to 1/6 Insurrection," *Just Security*, February 10, 2021.

Atlantic Council's Digital Forensic Research Lab, "360/Digital Sherlocks," webpage, undated. As of November 5, 2021: https://www.digitalsherlocks.org/360os-digitalsherlocks

Barari, Soubhik, Christopher Lucas, and Kevin Munger, "Political Deepfakes Are as Credible as Other Fake Media and (Sometimes) Real Media," unpublished manuscript, OSF Preprints, last updated April 16, 2021.

Brown, Nina I., "Deepfakes and the Weaponization of Disinformation," *Virginia Journal of Law and Technology*, Vol. 23, No. 1, 2020.

Brown, Tom B., Benjamin Mann, Nick Ryder, Melanie Subbiah, Jared Kaplan, Prafulla Dhariwal, Arvind Neelakantan, Pranav Shyam, Girish Sastry, Amanda Askell, et al., "Language Models Are Few-Shot Learners," unpublished manuscript, arXiv: 2005.14165v4, Version 4, last updated July 22, 2020.

C2PA—*See* Coalition for Content Provenance and Authenticity.

CAI—*See* Content Authenticity Initiative.

Coalition for Content Provenance and Authenticity, "Event Registration," webpage, January 26, 2022. As of February 15, 2022: https://c2pa.org/register/

———, "About," webpage, undated-a. As of February 15, 2022: https://c2pa.org/about/about/

———, "C2PA Specifications," webpage, undated-b. As of February 15, 2022: https://c2pa.org/public-draft/

Content Authenticity Initiative., "Addressing Misinformation Through Digital Content Provenance," webpage, undated-a. As of October 10, 2021: https://contentauthenticity.org

———, "How It Works," webpage, undated-b. As of April 30, 2022: https://contentauthenticity.org/how-it-works

California State Legislature, "Depiction of Individual Using Digital or Electronic Technology: Sexually Explicit Material: Cause of Action," Chapter 491, AB-602, October 4, 2019a.

———, "Elections: Deceptive Audio or Visual Media," Chapter 493, AB-730, October 4, 2019b.

Center for Countering Digital Hate, *The Disinformation Dozen: Why Platforms Must Act on Twelve Leading Online Anti-Vaxxers*, London, March 24, 2021.

Changsha Shenduronghe Network Technology, *ZAO*, mobile app, Zao App APK, September 1, 2019. As of October 10, 2021: https://zaodownload.com

Chesney, Bobby, and Danielle Citron, "Deep Fakes: A Looming Challenge for Privacy, Democracy, and National Security," *California Law Review*, Vol. 107, 2019, pp. 1753–1820.

Clayton, Katherine, et al., "Real Solutions for Fake News? Measuring the Effectiveness of General Warnings and Fact-Check Tags in Reducing Belief in False Stories on Social Media," *Political Behavior*, Vol. 42, No. 2, 2020, pp. 1073–1095.

Cole, Samantha, "This Horrifying App Undresses a Photo of Any Woman with a Single Click," *Vice*, June 26, 2019.

Collins, Ben, and Brandy Zadrozny, "How a Fake Persona Laid the Groundwork for a Hunter Biden Conspiracy Challenge," NBC News, October 29, 2020.

Committee on Homeland Security and Governmental Affairs, U.S. Senate, Deepfake Report Act of 2019, 116th Congress, S. Rept. 116-93, September 10, 2019.

Conspirador Norteño [@conspiratorO], "Xinjiang-related topics have been a perpetual target of astroturf campaigns ever since reports of human rights violations in the region emerged, and these accounts having identical 'conversations' about cotton production there are no exception [sic]," Twitter, October 18, 2021.

DelViscio, Jeffery, "A Nixon Deepfake, a 'Moon Disaster' Speech and an Information Ecosystem at Risk," *Scientific American*, July 20, 2020.

DiResta, Renée, "The Supply of Disinformation Will Soon Be Infinite," *The Atlantic*, September 20, 2020.

DiResta, Renee, Kris Shaffer, Becky Ruppel, David Sullivan, Robert Matney, Ryan Fox, Jonathan Albright, and Ben Johnson, *The Tactics and Tropes of the Internet Research Agency*, Austin, Tex.: New Knowledge, 2019.

"Ethiopia's Warring Sides Locked in Disinformation Battle," France 24, December 22, 2021. As of January 22, 2022:
https://www.france24.com/en/live-news/20211222-ethiopia-s-warring-sides-locked-in-disinformation-battle

Ferrer, Cristian Canton, Ben Pflaum, Jacqueline Pan, Brian Dolhansky, Joanna Bitton, and Jikuo Lu, "Deepfake Detection Challenge Results: An Open Initiative to Advance AI," Meta AI, blog, June 12, 2020. As of October 10, 2021:
https://ai.facebook.com/blog/deepfake-detection-challenge-results-an-open-initiative-to-advance-ai/

FireEye, "What Is a Zero-Day Exploit?" webpage, undated. As of January 20, 2022:
https://www.fireeye.com/current-threats/what-is-a-zero-day-exploit.html

Freedom House, "Countries and Territories," webpage, undated. As of January 20, 2022:
https://freedomhouse.org/countries/freedom-world/scores

Frenkel, Sheera, and Alba Davey, "In India, Facebook Grapples with an Amplified Version of Its Problems," *New York Times*, October 23, 2021.

Gamage, Dilrukshi, Jiayu Chen, and Kazutoshi Sasahara, "The Emergence of Deepfakes and Its Societal Implications: A Systematic Review," *Conference for Truth and Trust Online Proceedings*, October 2021.

Generated Photos, webpage, undated. As of November 10, 2021:
https://generated.photos/face-generator

Goldstein, Josh A., and Shelby Grossman, "How Disinformation Evolved in 2020," Brookings TechStream, January 4, 2021.

Goodfellow, Ian J., Jean Pouget-Abadie, Mehdi Mirza, Bing Xu, David Warde-Farley, Sherjil Ozair, Aaron Courville, and Yoshua Bengio, "Generative Adversarial Nets," in Z. Ghahramani, M. Welling, C. Cortes, N. Lawrence, and K. Q. Weinberger, eds., *Advances in Neural Information Processing Systems 27 Conference Proceedings (NIPS 2014)*, 2014, pp. 2672–2680.

Gregory, Sam, "Deepfakes and Synthetic Media: Survey of Solutions Against Malicious Usages," *Witness*, blog, undated. As of October 10, 2021:
https://blog.witness.org/2018/07/deepfakes-and-solutions/

Groh, Matthew, Ziv Epstein, Nick Obradovich, Manuel Cebrian, and Iyad Rahwan, "Human Detection of Machine-Manipulated Media," *Communications of the ACM*, Vol. 64, No. 10, 2022, pp. 40–47.

Guess, Andrew M., Michael Lerner, Benjamin Lyons, Jacob M. Montgomery, Brendan Nyhan, Jason Reifler, and Neelanjan Sircar, "A Digital Media Literacy Intervention Increases Discernment Between Mainstream and False News in the United States and India," *PNAS*, Vol. 117, No. 27, June 2020, pp. 15536–15545.

Gursky, Jacob, Martin J. Riedl, and Samuel Woolley, "The Disinformation Threat to Diaspora Communities in Encrypted Chat Apps," Brookings TechStream, March 19, 2021.

Hacker Factor, "Fotoforensics," homepage, undated. As of October 21, 2021:
http://fotoforensics.com

Halm, K. C., Ambika Kumar, Jonathan Segal, and Caeser Kalinowski IV, "Two California Laws Tackle Deepfake Videos in Politics and Porn," Davis Wright Tremaine LLP, October 14, 2019. As of October 30, 2021:
https://www.dwt.com/insights/2019/10/california-deepfakes-law

Hao, Karen, "Google Has Released a Giant Database of Deepfakes to Help Fight Deepfakes," *MIT Technology Review*, September 25, 2019.

Hao, Karen, "How Facebook and Google Fund Global Misinformation," *MIT Technology Review*, November 20, 2021.

Heaven, Will Douglas, "A GPT-3 Bot Posted Comments on Reddit for a Week and No One Noticed," *MIT Technology Review*, October 8, 2020.

Helmus, Todd C., and Marta Kepe, *A Compendium of Recommendations for Countering Russian and Other State-Sponsored Propaganda*, Santa Monica, Calif.: RAND Corporation, RR-A894-1, 2021. As of May 12, 2022:
https://www.rand.org/pubs/research_reports/RRA894-1.html

Helmus, Todd C., James V. Marrone, Marek N. Posard, and Danielle Schlang, *Russian Propaganda Hits Its Mark: Experimentally Testing the Impact of Russian Propaganda and Counter-Interventions*, Santa Monica, Calif.: RAND Corporation, RR-A704-3, 2020. As of March 25, 2022: https://www.rand.org/pubs/research_reports/RRA704-3.html

Hobantay Inc., *Celebrity Voice Cloning*, mobile app, undated. As of April 12, 2022: https://apps.apple.com/us/app/celebrity-voice-cloning/id1483201633

Huguet, Alice, Jennifer Kavanagh, Garrett Baker, and Marjory S. Blumenthal, *Exploring Media Literacy Education as a Tool for Mitigating Truth Decay*, Santa Monica, Calif.: RAND Corporation, RR-3050-RC, 2019. As of March 25, 2022: https://www.rand.org/pubs/research_reports/RR3050.html

Hwang, Tim, *Deepfakes: A Grounded Threat Assessment*, Washington, D.C.: Center for Security and Emerging Technology, Georgetown University, July 2020.

Hwang, Yoori, Ji Youn Ryu, and Se-Hoon Jeong, "Effects of Disinformation Using Deepfake: The Protective Effect of Media Literacy Education," *Cyberpsychology, Behavior, and Social Networking*, Vol. 24, No. 3, 2021, pp. 188–193.

Image Verification Assistant, homepage, undated. As of October 31, 2021: https://mever.iti.gr/forensics/

InVID and WeVerify, InVID, web browser plugin, Version 0.75.4, February 24, 2022. As of March 24, 2022: https://www.invid-project.eu/tools-and-services/invid-verification-plugin/

Jaiman, Ashish, "Media Literacy: An Effective Countermeasure for Deepfakes," *Medium*, blog, September 7, 2020. As of October 31, 2021: https://ashishjaiman.medium.com/media-literacy-an-effective-countermeasure-for-deepfakes-c6844c290857

Jankowicz, Nina, Jillian Hunchak, Alexandra Pavliuc, Celia Davies, Shannon Pierson, and Zoë Kaufmann, *Malign Creativity: How Gender, Sex and Lies Are Weaponized Against Women Online*, Washington, D.C.: Wilson Center, January 2021.

Johnson, Christian, *Deepfakes and Detection Technologies*, Santa Monica, Calif.: RAND Corporation, RR-A1482-1, forthcoming.

Kavanagh, Jennifer, and Michael D. Rich, *Truth Decay: An Initial Exploration of the Diminishing Role of Facts and Analysis in American Public Life*, Santa Monica, Calif.: RAND Corporation, RR-2314-RC, 2018. As of March 25, 2022: https://www.rand.org/pubs/research_reports/RR2314.html

Khodabakhsh, Ali, Raghavendra Ramachandra, and Christoph Busch, "Subjective Evaluation of Media Consumer Vulnerability to Fake Audiovisual Content," *Proceedings of 11th International Conference on Quality of Multimedia Experience (QoMEX)*, Berlin, Germany: IEEE, June 5–7, 2019.

Köbis, Nils C., Barbora Doležalová, and Ivan Soraperra, "Fooled Twice: People Cannot Detect Deepfakes but Think They Can," *iScience*, Vol. 24, No. 11, 2021.

Leibowicz, Claire, Jonathan Stray, and Emily Saltz, "Manipulated Media Detection Requires More Than Tools: Community Insights on What's Needed," Partnership on AI, blog post, July 13, 2020. As of October 21, 2021: https://partnershiponai.org/manipulated-media-detection-requires-more-than-tools-community-insights-on-whats-needed/

Li, Yuezun, Ming-Ching Chang, and Siwei Lyu, "In Ictu Oculi: Exposing AI Generated Fake Face Videos by Detecting Eye Blinking," unpublished manuscript, arXiv: 1806.02877v2, June 11, 2018.

Linvill, Darren, and Patrick Warren, "Understanding the Pro-China Propaganda and Disinformation Tool Set in Xinjiang," *Lawfare Blog*, December 1, 2021. As of June 6, 2022: https://www.lawfareblog.com/understanding-pro-china-propaganda-and-disinformation-tool-set-xinjiang

Marcellino, William, Todd C. Helmus, Joshua Kerrigan, Hilary Reininger, Rouslan I. Karimov, and Rebecca Ann Lawrence, *Detecting Conspiracy Theories on Social Media: Improving Machine Learning to Detect and Understand Online Conspiracy Theories*, Santa Monica, Calif.: RAND Corporation, RR-A676-1, 2021. As of March 25, 2022: https://www.rand.org/pubs/research_reports/RRA676-1.html

Meenu EG, "Try These 10 Amazingly Real Deepfake Apps and Websites," webpage, Analytics Insight, May 19, 2021. As of October 10, 2021: https://www.analyticsinsight.net/try-these-10-amazingly-real-deepfake-apps-and-websites/

Merriam-Webster, "deepfake," dictionary entry, undated-a. As of March 25, 2022: https://www.merriam-webster.com/dictionary/deepfake

Merriam-Webster, "disinformation," dictionary entry, undated-b. As of April 25, 2022: https://www.merriam-webster.com/dictionary/disinformation

Merriam-Webster, "misinformation," dictionary entry, undated-c. As of April 25, 2022: https://www.merriam-webster.com/dictionary/misinformation

MIT Open Learning, "Tackling the Misinformation Epidemic with 'In Event of Moon Disaster,'" webpage, MIT News, July 20, 2020. As of October 10, 2021:
https://news.mit.edu/2020/mit-tackles-misinformation-in-event-of-moon-disaster-0720

MyHeritage, homepage, undated. As of October 10, 2021:
https://www.myheritage.com

Networking and Information Technology Research and Development, "About the Networking and Information Technology Research and Development (NITRD) Program," webpage, undated. As of January 31, 2022:
https://www.nitrd.gov/about/

Nimmo, Ben, C. Shawn Eib, L. Tamora, Kate Johnson, Ian Smith, Eto Buziashvili, Alyssa Kann, Kanishk Karan, Esteban Ponce de León Rosas, and Max Rizzuto, #OperationFFS: Fake Face Swarm, Graphika and Atlantic Council's Digital Forensic Research Lab, December 2019.

Nyhan, Brendan, Ethan Porter, Jason Reifler, and Thomas J. Wood, "Taking Fact-Checks Literally but Not Seriously? The Effects of Journalistic Fact-Checking on Factual Beliefs and Candidate Favorability," Political Behavior, Vol. 42, September 2020, pp. 939–960.

O'Sullivan, Donie, "Doctored Videos Shared to Make Pelosi Sound Drunk Viewed Millions of Times on Social Media," CNN, May 24, 2019.

Pennycook, Gordon, Adam Bear, Evan Collins, and David G. Rand, "The Implied Truth Effect: Attaching Warnings to a Subset of Fake News Stories Increases Perceived Accuracy of Stories Without Warnings," Management Science, August 2019.

Pennycook, Gordon, Ziv Epstein, Mohsen Mosleh, Antonio A. Arechar, Dean Eckles, and David G. Rand, "Shifting Attention to Accuracy Can Reduce Misinformation Online," Nature, Vol. 592, 2021, pp. 590–595.

Posard, Marek N., Marta Kepe, Hilary Reininger, James V. Marrone, Todd C. Helmus, and Jordan R. Reimer, From Consensus to Conflict: Understanding Foreign Measures Targeting U.S. Elections, Santa Monica, Calif.: RAND Corporation, RR-A704-1, 2020. As of March 31, 2022:
https://www.rand.org/pubs/research_reports/RRA704-1.html

Reface, homepage, undated. As of October 10, 2021:
https://hey.reface.ai

Reuters Communications, "Reuters Expands Deepfake Course to 16 Languages in Partnership with Facebook Journalism Project," Reuters Press Blog, June 15, 2020. As of November 20, 2021:
https://www.reuters.com/article/rpb-fbdeepfakecourselanguages/reuters-expands-deepfake-course-to-16-languages-in-partnership-with-facebook-journalism-project-idUSKBN23M1QY

"[A] Robot Wrote This Entire Article. Are You Scared Yet, Human?" The Guardian, September 8, 2020. As of October 10, 2021:
https://www.theguardian.com/commentisfree/2020/sep/08/robot-wrote-this-article-gpt-3

Rushing, Ellie, "A Philly Lawyer Nearly Wired $9,000 to a Stranger Impersonating His Son's Voice, Showing Just How Smart Scammers Are Getting," Philadelphia Enquirer, March 9, 2020.

Sablayrolles, Alexandre, Matthijs Douze, Cordelia Schmid, and Hervé Jégou, "Radioactive Data: Tracing Through Training," unpublished manuscript, arXiv: 2002.00937, February 3, 2020.

Satter, Raphael, "Experts: Spy Used AI-Generated Face to Connect with Targets," AP News, June 13, 2019.

Sayler, Kelley M., and Laurie A. Harris, "Deep Fakes and National Security," Congressional Research Service, updated June 8, 2021.

Shane, Tommy, Emily Saltz, and Claire Leibowicz, "From Deepfakes to TikTok Filters: How Do You Label AI Content?" Nieman Lab, May 12, 2021.

Shen, Tianxiang, Ruixian Liu, Ju Bai, and Zheng Li, "'Deep Fakes' Using Generative Adversarial Networks (GAN)," Noiselab, University of California, San Diego, 2018. As of October 10, 2021:
http://noiselab.ucsd.edu/ECE228_2018/Reports/Report16.pdf

Shin, Jieun, "How Do Partisans Consume News on Social Media? A Comparison of Self-Reports with Digital Trace Measures Among Twitter Users," Social Media + Society, Vol. 6, No. 4, December 2020.

Simonite, Tom, "To See the Future of Disinformation, You Build Robo-Trolls," Wired, November 19, 2019.

———, "What Happened to the Deepfake Threat to the Election?" Wired, November 16, 2020.

Singh, Simranjeet, Rajneesh Sharma, and Alan F. Smeaton, "Using GANs to Synthesize Minimum Training Data for Deepfake Generation," unpublished manuscript, arXiv: 2011.05421, November 10, 2020.

Sprout Social, "Meme," webpage, undated. As of January 22, 2022:
https://sproutsocial.com/glossary/meme/

Stamos, Alex, Sergey Sanovich, Andrew Grotto, and Allison Berke, "Combatting Organized Disinformation Campaigns from State-Aligned Actors," in Michael McFaul, ed., Securing American Elections: Prescriptions for Enhancing the Integrity and Independence of the 2020 U.S. Presidential Election and Beyond, Stanford, Calif.: Freeman Spogli Institute for International Studies, Stanford University, 2019, pp. 43–52.

Starling Lab, "78 Days: The Archive," webpage, undated. As of November 10, 2021:
https://www.starlinglab.org/78daysarchive/

Stewart, Emily, "Trump Has Started Suggesting the *Access Hollywood* Tape Is Fake. It's Not." *Vox*, November 28, 2017.

Stoll, Ashley, "Shallowfakes and Their Potential for Fake News," *Washington Journal of Law, Technology, and Arts*, January 13, 2020.

Stupp, Catherine, "Fraudsters Used AI to Mimic CEO's Voice in Unusual Cybercrime Case," *Wall Street Journal*, August 30, 2019.

Tanasi, Alessandro, and Marco Buoncristiano, Ghiro, homepage, 2017. As of October 31, 2021:
https://www.getghiro.org

Texas State Legislature, an act relating to the creation of a criminal offense for fabricating a deceptive video with intent to influence the outcome of an election, TX SB-751, introduced June 14, 2019.

Tom [@deeptomcruise], "Sports!" TikTok, February 22, 2021. As of November 10, 2021:
https://www.tiktok.com/@deeptomcruise/video/6932166297996233989

U.S. House of Representatives, DEEP FAKES Accountability Act, 116th Congress, H.R. 3230, referred to Committees on Judiciary, Energy and Commerce, and Homeland Security, June 28, 2019.

U.S. Senate, Malicious Deep Fake Prohibition Act, S. 3805, 115th Congress, referred to the Committee on the Judiciary, December 21, 2018.

———, National Defense Authorization Act for Fiscal Year 2020, Public Law 116-92, December 20, 2020. As of June 5, 2022:
https://www.govinfo.gov/content/pkg/PLAW-116publ92/html/PLAW-116publ92.htm

———, Deepfake Task Force Act, S. 2559, May 24, 2022.

Vaccari, Cristian, and Andrew Chadwick, "Deepfakes and Disinformation: Exploring the Impact of Synthetic Political Video on Deception, Uncertainty, and Trust in News," *Social Media + Society*, Vol. 6, No. 1, January 2020.

Victor, Daniel, "Your Loved Ones, and Eerie Tom Cruise Videos, Reanimate Unease with Deepfakes," *New York Times*, March 10, 2021.

Vincent, James, "Watch Jordan Peele Use AI to Make Barack Obama Deliver a PSA About Fake News," *The Verge*, April 17, 2018.

———, "Tom Cruise Deepfake Creator Says Public Shouldn't Be Worried About 'One-Click Fakes,'" *The Verge*, March 5, 2021.

Voloshchuk, Alexander, *Voicer Famous AI Voice Changer*, mobile app, Version 1.17.5, Apple App Store, undated. As of November 10, 2021:
https://apps.apple.com/us/app/voicer-famous-ai-voice-changer/id1484480839

Waldemarsson, Christoffer, *Disinformation, Deepfakes and Democracy: The European Response to Election Interference in the Digital Age*, Copenhagen: Alliance of Democracies, April 27, 2020.

Walorska, Agnieszka M., *Deepfakes and Disinformation*, Postdam, Germany: Friedrich Naumann Foundation for Freedom, 2020.

Walter, Nathan, John J. Brooks, Camille J. Saucier, and Sapna Suresh, "Evaluating the Impact of Attempts to Correct Health Misinformation on Social Media: A Meta-Analysis," *Health Communication*, Vol. 36, No. 13, 2020, pp. 1776–1784.

Washington Post, "Seeing Isn't Believing: The Fact Checker's Guide to Manipulated Video," webpage, undated. As of November 20, 2021:
https://www.washingtonpost.com/graphics/2019/politics/fact-checker/manipulated-video-guide/

Wasike, Ben, "Memes, Memes, Everywhere, nor Any Meme to Trust: Examining the Credibility and Persuasiveness of COVID-19-Related Memes," *Journal of Computer-Mediated Communication*, Vol. 27, No. 2, March 2022.

Wittenberg, Chloe, Ben M. Tappin, Adam J. Berinsky, and David G. Rand, "The (Minimal) Persuasive Advantage of Political Video over Text," *Proceedings of the National Academy of Sciences*, Vol. 118, No. 47, 2021.

Wong, Sui-Lin, Christian Shepherd, and Qianer Liu, "Old Messages, New Memes: Beijing's Propaganda Playbook on the Hong Kong Protests," *Financial Times*, September 3, 2019.

World Population Review, "Literacy Rate by Country 2022," webpage, undated. As of January 20, 2022:
https://worldpopulationreview.com/country-rankings/literacy-rate-by-country

Yaqub, Waheeb, Otari Kakhidze, Morgan L. Brockman, Nasir Memon, and Sameer Patil, "Effects of Credibility Indicators on Social Media News Sharing Intent," *CHI Conference on Human Factors in Computing Systems Proceedings*, Honolulu: ACM, April 25–30, 2020.

Yu, Ning, Vladislav Skripniuk, Sahar Abdelnabi, and Mario Fritz, "Artificial Fingerprinting for Generative Models: Rooting Deepfake Attribution in Training Data," unpublished manuscript, arXiv: 2007.08457v6, October 7, 2021.